This guide is dedicated to the amazing CM and VM of Team Adventure. I couldn't be more proud of you both.

Always brave. Ever, ever, ever.

Forever in my heart - Dad

Disclaimer:

The Legend of Zelda is a registered trademark of Nintendo. The screenshots and artwork shown in this publication were taken from "The Legend of Zelda: Link's Awakening", a game developed and published by Nintendo.

This educational guide is a 100% independent and unofficial publication which is in no way, licensed, authorized, or endorsed by Nintendo. This guide book is for general information and entertainment purposes only.

Names, brands, and logos mentioned within this publication may be protected by trademark or other intellectual property rights of one or more jurisdictions. It is not implied that there is any commercial, or other relationship, between the publisher and the trademark holder.

The strategy guide text and layout is Copyright © 2020 - 2022 by Alpha Strategy Guides.

All rights reserved.

No part of this book may be reproduced in any form, or by electronic or mechanical means, including information storage and retrieval systems, without the expressed written permission from the author ("Alpha Strategy Guides"), except for the use of brief quotations in a book review.

ISBN: 9781739902377

Printed in the UK

Table of Contents

Chapter 1 - The Requirements for 100%...	11
Chapter 2 - Our top tips for beginners...	12
"Bomb Arrows" - A blast from Link's past	12
Crazy cheap extra life	12
Spin to win	12
Chapter 3 - From classic to (Re)remake	13
Chapter 4 - The Journey to the first dungeon	14
Waking Up	14
Go grab your sword	14
The Mysterious Forest	15
Making the Magic Powder	17
Finding the Dungeon Key	17
First Dungeon: Tail Cave	18
Mini-Boss: Spike Roller	20
Nightmare Boss Fight: Moldorm	21
Chapter 5 - The Journey to the second dungeon	22
To Goponga Swamp	22
Let's Rescue BowWoW	22
Moblin Mini-Boss	23
To the Second Dungeon	23
Second Dungeon: Bottle Grotto	24
Mini-Boss: Hinox	26
Nightmare Boss Fight	29
Chapter 6 - The Journey to the third dungeon	30
Taking BowWow Back Home	30
Magic Powder Upgrade	30

Mabe Village Item Bonanza	32
To Kanalet Castle	33
Kanalet Castle and the Five Golden Leaves	36
Side-Quest Rewards and the Dungeon Key	37
Third Dungeon: Key Cavern	39
Mini-Boss: Dodongo Snakes	40
Nightmare Boss Fight	42

Chapter 7 - The Journey to the fourth dungeon — 43

To the Dream Shrine	43
To the Color Dungeon	44
The Color Dungeon	46
Mini-Boss: Giant Buzz Blob	46
Mini-Boss: Avalaunch	47
Boss: Hardhit Beetle	48
Item Collect-a-thon	50
Open the Path to Yarna Desert	52
Retrieving the Fourth Dungeon Key	53
Opening the Fourth Dungeon	54
To the Fourth Dungeon	55
Fourth Dungeon: Angler's Tunnel	56
Mini-Boss: Hydrosoar	57
Nightmare Boss Fight	59

Chapter 8 - The Journey to the fifth dungeon — 60

Item Collect-a-thon	60

Next Major Item: Bow and Arrow Set	64
To the Fifth Dungeon	66
Fifth Dungeon: Catfish's Maw	68
Mini-Boss: Master Stalfos (Part 1)	68
Mini-Boss: Master Stalfos (Part 2)	69
Mini-Boss: Master Stalfos (Part 3)	69
Mini-Boss: Master Stalfos (Part 4)	69
Mini-Boss: Gohma	70
Nightmare Boss Fight (Slime Eel)	71

Chapter 9 - The Journey to the sixth dungeon — 72

Completing the Trade Sub-Quest	72
To the Ancient Ruins	72
Ancient Ruins	74
Mini-Boss: Amos Knight	75
Sixth Dungeon: Face Shrine	77
Mini-Boss: Rover	79
Mini-Boss: Dodongo Snakes	80
Nightmare Boss Fight	81

Chapter 10 - The Journey to the seventh dungeon — 82

Riding the Rapid Rafts	82
Rapids Raid	82
Rapids Race	84
The Final Ocarina Song	85
Seashell and Heart Piece Bonanza	87

To the Next Dungeon's Key	93
To the Eagle's Tower Dungeon	94
Seventh Dungeon: Eagle's Tower	95
Mini-Boss: Hinox	97
Mini-Boss: The Grim Creeper	98
Nightmare Boss Fight	98
Chapter 11 - The Journey to the eighth dungeon	99
To Turtle Rock	99
Eighth Dungeon: Turtle Rock	102
Mini-Boss: Hinox	102
Mini-Boss: Spike Roller	102
Mini-Boss: Rover	103
Mini-Boss: Dodongo Snakes	105
Mini-Boss: Blaino	105
Mini-Boss: Hydrosoar	106
Nightmare Boss Fight	108
Chapter 12 - Before beating the final boss...	109
Chamber Stones 1 and 2	109
Chamber Stones 3 - 9	109
Chamber Stones 10 and 11	110
Chamber Stones 12 and 13	110
Chamber Stone 14	110
Chapter 13 - The Final Challenge	111
You're almost there...	111

Side Mission: Trendy Figures	113
En-route to the Egg	113
Final Dungeon: The Wind Fish's Egg	114
Final Boss: Shadow Nightmare	114
Shadow Nightmare: Form 1	114
Shadow Nightmare: Form 2	114
Shadow Nightmare: Form 3	115
Shadow Nightmare: Form 4	115
Shadow Nightmare: Form 5	116
Shadow Nightmare: Final Form (Dethl)	116

Chapter 14 - Secrets and Easter Eggs — 117

Hidden Music	117
Bomb Arrows	117
Death by a Thousand Pecks	117
THIEF!	118
Cameos	118
Hidden Marin Dialogue	119
Fun with the Magic Powder	120
Relived Nightmares	120
Say Cheese!	121

Chapter 15 - Hearts and Seashell locations — 124

Heart Piece Locations Map	124
Secret Seashell Locations Map	126

Introduction

Welcome to the majestic world of Koholint Island. Originally released in 1993, this Zelda game was simply mesmerizing and it's a game that easily in our top five games of all time (the nostalgia and amazing memories is very strong with this game).

How Nintendo managed to cram so much content, so many secrets, and so much emotion into that original Gameboy cartridge is beyond us. The gameplay, the music, the characters, everything about it was simply incredible.

Then the Gameboy Color DX ("Deluxe") upgrade released in 1998 added an extra dungeon (also found in this Switch remake), the ability to trigger some "Kodak moments" and then, quite literally, print them out on the Gameboy Printer accessory. Fun times.

Now, we've got a completely remade version of the game and it certainly hasn't lost any of its charm (in fact, it's managed to add some more charm with its new graphical style). The characters we know and love are still there, new ones have been introduced, new puzzles, new collectables, new challenges, and an amazingly orchestral music score. And, yet, it still feels like the Link's Awakening that we grew up with all those years ago.

So, it's fair to say that we absolutely loved playing through this game again in the name of creating this strategy guide for you. Even if you've played the originals, there's enough new content (including a large increase in collectables), to get stuck into and enjoy.

All of us at Alpha Strategy Guides truly hope that this as-spoiler-free-as-possible strategy guide compliments your playthrough by removing your frustrations.

Enjoy.

Alpha Strategy Guides

Chapter 1

The Requirements for 100%...

Here's what you need to find and collect if you're aiming for that elusive 100% completion rate:

- Find and collect all 32 Heart Containers.
- Find and collect all 50 Secret Seashells.
- Find and collect all 3 Fairy Bottles.
- Obtain the Boomerang.
- Upgrade Arrow capacity to 60 arrows.
- Upgrade Bomb capacity to 60 bombs.
- Upgrade the Magic Powder capacity to 40.
- Collect all 10 Figurines at the Trendy Game.
- Collect all Stone Beaks.
- Unlock all 10 Warp Points.
- Complete the Color Dungeon.
- Complete all 24 Chamber Dungeons.
- Find and collect all 14 Chamber Stones.
- Find and collect all 6 amiibo Chambers.
- Collect the extra Small Key in Key Cavern.
- Finally, clear the game without dying (unlocks the hidden "best" ending).

Chapter 2

Our top tips for beginners...

One of the benefits of following a strategy guide like ours, is that you get the benefit of our experience and hindsight. With that in mind, here's a few tips that we reckon will serve you well and you enjoy making your way around Koholint Island.

"Bomb Arrows" - A blast from Link's past

Bomb Arrows were available in the original Gameboy release of Link's Awakening, which was effectively a glitch from the first Zelda game. After equipping both the arrows and bombs, press both buttons at the same time!

All of a sudden, Link would fire off an Arrow with a bomb attached to the front of it. Not only did this look cool, but the bomb also exploded on impact! This could be used to quickly blow up rocks in the distance, or to detonate bombs without waiting for the fuse to go off.

This trick is available in the remake (which is a nice nod, as the developers could have easily removed it), but you need to be very careful. If the explosion hits you, then Link loses two full hearts!

Crazy cheap extra life

It's not just bottled faeries that can bring you back to life in this game. Make your way to Crazy Tracy's Health Spa (located left of Tabahl Wasteland) and, for only 28 rupees, she'll apply a special cream that will automatically bring you back to life if you ever lose all of your hearts! Be sure to go back to her if you happen to lose a life to get the special cream reapplied again.

Spin to win

As soon as you pick up the sword off of the beach, start holding the attack button down to charge your sword up. Once the sword is fully charged, let go of the attack  button to unleash a move that's not only twice as powerful as a regular attack, but... it also damages every enemy around you that's close by. Sweet!

12

Chapter 3

From classic to (Re)remake

The original Gameboy version of Link's Awakening was released in North America on August 6th 1993. Allegedly, it originally began creation as a side-project from within Nintendo of Japan, and it only became an official, Nintendo-approved project after the release of the legendary "A Link to the Past" on the Super Nintendo in 1991.

The game then got a re-release for the Gameboy Color on December 15th 1998 in North America, under the title: Link's Awakening DX. Not only was this cartridge backwards compatible with the original Gameboy, but it also included a hidden extra color-based dungeon that made use of the Gameboy Color's color screen (but was unavailable if the DX cartridge was played in an original Gameboy console).

The DX version also included an exclusive character that took photographs of Link at key locations on the map. These photos could not only be viewed on the screen (at his shop) but, if you also owned a Gameboy Printer, you could connect it to your Gameboy (Color) and physically print those photos out in real-life! (Which are available to see on page **121**).

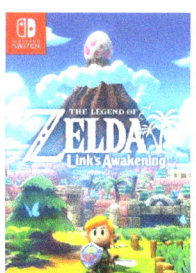

Finally, this brings us to the release of the Switch remake. A complete overhaul with the same DX-exclusive dungeon, but the photographic mouse has been removed (and has been replaced by challenge dungeons instead). Just as captivating as the 1993 original release.

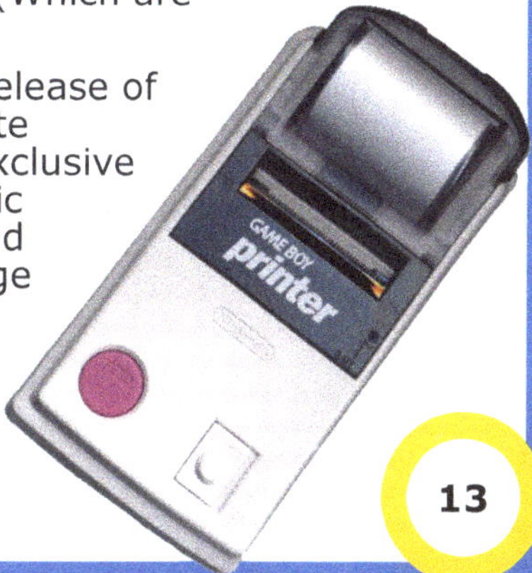

13

Chapter 4

The Journey to the first dungeon

Waking Up

Once you've woken up and have spoken with Marin, jump out of bed and immediately speak with her father Tarin. He'll give you back your Shield! With your shield in hand, leave Marin's house and you'll reappear in **Mabe Village**.

Immediately head left, walk down past the BowWow that's chained up to the wooden post and follow the yellow path South.

Drop down the gaps in the ledges, dodging the rocks fired by the Octoroks, and you'll land on the sandy beach of **Toronbo Shores**.

Go grab your sword

Walk right, dodge the black **Sea Urchin** in your way, then press the R button to lift your shield. With your shield raised, walk into one of the two Sea Urchins that block your path to the lighter sand. You can push this enemy away with your shield and you won't take any damage while doing so.

Now head right, push the next Sea Urchin out of the way, and go South towards the water. In here you'll find your **Sword**! Walk into the water, chat to Owl, and then pick it up!

Now you have both your shield and your sword in-hand, it's time to begin the adventure properly.

Head up and use your sword on all nearby enemies. Killing them will often reward you with a Rupee.

Rupees can come in different colors, each one worth a different value:

- *Green* = 1 rupee,
- *Blue* = 5 rupees,
- *Red* = 20 rupees,
- *Purple* = 50 rupees,
- *Silver* = 100 rupees,
- *Gold* = 300 rupees.

Make your way up and to the left, heading back the way you originally came. When you see BowWow, continue up, and then look left for a ledge that overlooks a square hole.

Hack the bushes away and then drop down into the hole. You'll land in a cave with the game's first **Heart Piece**! Once collected, climb the stairs to reappear back in Mabe Village. Immediately proceed Northwards and hack away the bush that's blocking the path to reach the Mysterious Forest.

Heart Piece 01/32

Drop into the well, opposite the library.

(Mabe Village)

Collected?

The Mysterious Forest

Once Owl has finished talking, go up and you'll encounter a new enemy, **Mobilns**. These enemies take two hits from your sword to kill. You can also hold up your shield to block their spear attack.

Go right, take out the Moblin and then run through the narrow opening to the right of the screen. Continue going right, dispose of the next Moblin and then enter the tree trunk to reappear inside a cave with a chest in it (along with some bats known as **Keese**).

Couple of things to note here:

1. The purple crystals only take one sword swipe to break.
2. The cracks on the floor indicate weak sections. So, keep moving as you run over them. Otherwise, Link will fall into the hole that appears, costing you half a heart every time this happens.

With that in mind, to open the chest, kill the bats with a charged sword attack as they get close (bearing in mind that you can still walk, although more slowly, when charging your sword).

15

Smash the first set of crystals, run along the top of the room and down to the regular ground. Smash the next set of crystals and then push the rock left, giving you access to the chest. Open it to obtain a **Purple Rupee** worth **50 rupees**!

Continue North, and you'll come across a new enemy, the **Green Zol**. These enemies aren't difficult to deal with, just hit them fast with rapid swings of your sword.

When you enter the next room, ignore the Heart Piece that's sitting there. You can't get it (yet). So, push the rock below you down one space and then the next rock to your left one space to open up a path to the exit in the middle of the room.

When you reappear back in the **Mysterious Forest**, you'll see a Moblin that has a sword and shield. Hold up your shield and let it attack first. It'll stagger itself for a few seconds, leaving it open for an easy counter-attack.

Now cut the bushes down on the left and pick up the **Toadstool** that's sitting on the ground (**Note:** NOT something we recommend you do for real – unless you have a genuine knowledge of fungi).

Now, go back into the wooden tree stump you came out of and make your way back through the cave until you're back in the **Mysterious Forest** (with the sign on your left).

Dispose of the Moblin and then go up. Take out the sword and shield Moblin and then continue North. Be careful of the two red Gels as they split into two smaller Gels when you hack them to pieces. Lots of quick sword swipes will help you here.

Ignore the dark grey rocks (for now) and go up and fight your way past the Moblins to enter a new area, **Koholint Prairie**.

16

Making the Magic Powder

Continue South, and you'll come across a new enemy, the **Buzz Blob**. *Do not* attack them if you see them charging with electricity. Doing so only hurts you and costs you some precious health. Instead, attack them when they're not covered in electricity.

Keep going down and then enter the spooky looking tree with the skull on its roof. Inside, speak to the **Witch** and give her the **Toadstool** so she can conjure up some special **Magic Powder** for you. Awesome!

Magic Powder

The Magic Powder can be used to: Light torches, defeat some enemies, and it can even remove the magic spell off of anyone who was silly enough to eat one of those Toadstools...

Keep in mind that Magic Powder can only be used a set number of times before it runs out. For more powder, collect another Toadstool and take it back to the Witch to make more.

Finding the Dungeon Key

Go back outside and it's time to go North and back into the Mysterious Forest. Go left, past the Moblins, then down, then left again at the gap between the trees, and now go up.

When you see the **Raccoon** standing by the tree, sprinkle some Magic Powder on it to turn it into Tarin! What a silly man!

With that task complete, go North and open up the chest here for the **Tail Key** (which you'll use soon). It's now time to go South and back towards Mabe Village.

With that all-important key in hand, continue down towards the beach area again. Although, this time, continue to the right side (sticking to the Northern path, past all of the Octoroks), and you'll soon reach the entrance to the first dungeon. Use your key in the middle pillar to open up the entrance.

17

Dungeon One – Tail Cave

Immediately upon entering the game's first dungeon, go left and use your sword to knock the two **Hardhat Beetles** off of the platform and to their doom. A **Small Key** magically drops down from the ground onto the gray path. Be sure to pick it up!

Note: Small keys can only be used once to open up a regular locked door.

When entering the next room, be ready to quickly dispose of the **Green Zols**. But also watch out for the fire lanterns that shoot fireballs at your general direction!

Dodge these and then open the chest for a **Compass**. Go right two screens, then up one. Dispose of the enemies in here and stand on the switch to reveal a chest. Open it to collect a **Small Key**.

Go right and immediately begin charging your sword. Use charged attacks on the two **Stalfos** skeletons that get up from the floor. Clear out the **Keese** to reveal a **hidden chest**. Inside you'll obtain the **Map**.

Go up, use a charge attack on the enemies here and use a small key to unlock the door to the right. Dodge the two yellow **Sparks** that circle the room, while using a charged attack on the Stalfos that gets up.

Go North and then in this room your goal is to strike the enemies (known as **Three-of-a-Kind**), so they all have the same symbol showing.

Each symbol appears for a second, so be quick on your attacks. If you fail, leave the room, and reenter it to reset the enemies for another attempt.

Note

The beak can be used on an Owl statue that has its beak missing (such as the one that's - conveniently - located at the top of this room!), for some hints and tips.

18

Match all three to reveal a Stone Beak.

Go south, then left, and proceed further left. You'll encounter more Sparks but also a **Mini-Moldorm**.

Carefully use charged attacks on this (while dodging the Sparks as they circle around the chest). Open the chest for a Small Key.

Be sure to dispose of the next Mini-Moldorm to your left to reveal a **hidden chest** that contains a **Red Rupee** worth a useful 20 rupees.

Go up and be careful of the **Blade Trap** that spins across the floor when you get close. Wait for it to move left again before opening the locked door ahead.

In the next room, run right, dodge the enemies and when you reach the Owl statue near the locked door, push the wooden square, that's facing opposite the Owl statue, to the right to unlock the door.

To defeat the **Spiked Beetles** in here, hold up your shield and when they charge at you they'll flip over after hitting your shield. Now finish them off with your sword. Proceed down the steps that appear in the top-right corner of the room.

It's time for some classic 2D side-scrolling action! Be careful as you can't jump – yet – so use your swords on the **Goombas** and climb the ladders until you reappear in a long corridor. It's time to collect a new upgrade!

Proceed North and bait the two **Blade Traps** into hitting each other before you go up to the chest and open it to collect the **Roc's Feather**.

Roc's Feather

The Roc's Feather gives Link the ability to jump over small gaps. Easily one of the most useful (and most used) items in the game.

After assigning the feather to a button, you can press this button to make Link leap up into the air. Which, as per the usual rules of game design, can be used to leap over the two Blade Traps and also to collect the **floating Three Hearts** that's hovering around the corridor. It also allows you to leap across gaps! How handy is that!?

19

Go back down the stairs, jump across to the ladder leading up, go right, and then use your feather to jump across the gap at the bottom (removing the need to dodge those Sparks again).

In the next room, go down and then to the right (towards the open chest). When you reach the row of blocks, navigate to the upper portion of the blocks, and then jump across the gap to the block with the keyhole in it.

Use one of your small keys to open the block, go up the steps, and then open up the chest for that all-important **Nightmare Key** (which is needed to open up the door to the boss room).

Go back down and across the gap, go left, and then right at the split in the blocks. Continue right, stick to the Southern wall (to dodge the Sparks), and jump across the gap. Enter the door, to face-off against your first mini-boss!

Mini-Boss: Spike Roller

This mini-boss requires a total of eight hits from your sword to go down. The trick here is to jump over the spiked roller as it's pushed towards you and try to hit the creature two or three times as it bounces across to the other side of the room.

While it's not overly difficult, just be mindful that the roller speeds up each time it reaches the other side of the room.

Defeating the mini-boss achieves three things:

1. All locked doors are now open.

2. A Fairy appears. Jumping into a Fairy automatically replenishes **all** of your health.

3. A portal is created in the middle of the room. This portal acts as a shortcut between the entrance of the dungeon and this room.

Here's a pre-warning, *before* entering the Northern door, be ready to **leap into the air** to dodge the two Blade Traps that are sneakily waiting for you as soon as you enter the next room! Cheeky!

Use the **Nightmare Key** on the locked door in here to begin the game's first main boss fight!

Moldorm

Nightmare Boss Fight: Moldorm

The trick to quickly beating this boss is to hit the red ball at the end of its tail with a charge sword attack. Hitting the red ball causes the boss to dramatically speed up. Attempting to hit the boss anywhere else will be a waste of time. However, you can't hit the tail while the ball is covered by the flower petals. You must wait for it to appear for the boss to be vulnerable.

It only requires two successful charged sword attacks on the red ball to finish off the boss for good.

Your rewards are a **Heart Container** and, in the next room, the **Full Moon Cello**! Sweet!

Did You Know?

Moldorm has also appeared as a boss in the SNES "A Link to the Past" and in the 3DS release "A Link Between Worlds."

21

Chapter 5

The Journey to the second dungeon

To Goponga Swamp

Once Link walks back outside and has spoken to the Owl, it's time to head back to Mabe Village. Once you're told the bad news, proceed immediately to the **Mysterious Forest**.

Head to the right, through the small gap in the trees, then head up, take a right at the three stones, and then you'll be in **Koholint Prairie**. Use the feather to leap across the gap to claim your second **Heart Piece**!

Heart Piece 02/32

Near the Mysterious Forest exit.

(Koholint Prairie)

Collected?

With the Heart Piece in your possession, jump across the gap to the North and then you'll enter a new area called **Tal Tal Heights**.

Let's Rescue BowWow

Proceed to the right and head inside the doorway with the Moblin statue. Once inside, use your shield to block the Moblin's attack and counter with your sword when it's off-balance.

The next room contains four spear-throwing Moblins. Keep to the tried-and-tested block and counter move and take them on one-at-a-time (unless you're confident with your charged sword attacks). Now enter the next room.

Top Tip!

Picking up a Guardian Acorn halves the amount of damage you take. Collecting a Triforce Piece doubles your sword damage. However, you can only use one at a time.

22

Moblin Mini-Boss

This mini-boss has a slow and predictable pattern. He'll throw an unblock-able giant spear at you. So, move out of the way, then stand in front of the closed door. This baits the large Moblin to charge at you (which is signaled by it beating its chest first). If you're not standing close to the door, then the Moblin may stop running, preventing him from hitting the wall and stunning himself.

Move down and out of the way. The Moblin is only vulnerable to your attacks when you see the stars spinning around its head (which only lasts for a few seconds – so be quick with your sword attacks!). It takes a total of **eight** successful hits to take the mini-boss down for good.

 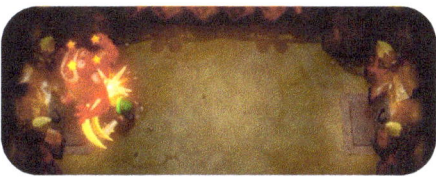

Now enter the open door on the right, approach **BowWow** and press **A** to bring the gentle metallic ball of sharp teeth with you.

Exit the Moblin hideout, speak with Owl, then leave **Tal Tal Heights** the way you came by going left, then down. Jump across the gap to where the heart piece was and go left towards the **Mysterious Woods**.

You'll be pleased to hear that BowWow has got quite the appetite and will gladly much on any enemies it encounters along the way. Which is handy.

Keep going go the left and jump across the gap to the open chest. Go up and left, then go up again, take a right, and you'll soon step into the start of Goponga Swamp.

To the Second Dungeon

Go up, then right and attack the flower to make BowWow eat it up, opening up the path ahead. Keep going right and then let BowWow eat the **Giant Goponga Flowers** that are in your way. Go down towards the chest and open it for a handy **Purple Rupee** worth **50 rupees**.

Go up to the wall at the top and then to the right. Attack the flowers that surround the entrance to the cave and BowWow will gladly clear a path for you. How helpful!

Second Dungeon: Bottle Grotto

When you enter this dungeon, you'll notice a chest surrounded by a lot of jars. You can't destroy these pots just yet. But, as in true Zelda game fashion, you'll acquire an item in this dungeon that will help. For now, move North into the next room.

Use the **Magic Powder** on both of the unlit torches to light them and open up the doorway on the right. Now dispose of the regular **Stalfos** and the **Yellow Stalfos** that jumps to your last location. Once they're gone, collect the **Small Key** that drops down to the ground.

Go left, open the locked door, and **STOP!** Let the two Blade Traps hit, and then walk, or jump past them. Take out both **Keese** bats and then head North.

Light the two torches in the next room and then leap across the gap at a 45-degree angle (allowing you to get behind the **Hardhat Beetle**). Hit it until it falls off and then open the chest to obtain the **Stone Beak** for this dungeon.

Go back down into the previous room (remembering to wait for the Blade Traps at the entrance of the door), keep going right and you'll eventually enter into a room with an Owl statue and a large blue crystal.

Head down and watch out for the shield-carrying **Sword Stalfos** and block its attacks before hitting it with your sword. Now hit the orange crystal to grant you access to the chest. Open it to collect the **Small Key**.

Note

Hitting the crystal when it is blue drops all blue blocks, but also raises all orange blocks.

Keep this in mind as you progress through the puzzles in this dungeon.

With that in mind, hit the crystal when it's **blue** to drop the blocks at the top of the room. Before you leave this room, hit the **orange** crystal to turn it blue. Now proceed to the left, head down, and open up the locked door.

24

Puzzle time! The **Shy Guy** in this room moves in the opposite direction to where you move. So, for example, if you move left, it'll move to the right. Keep things simple by lining yourself up with the left-hand side of the pots and face the left-hand wall. Now start charging up a spinning attack and very slowly move up and to the right.

Once you're within range, unleash your spinning attack and dispose of it, revealing a chest. Open the chest for this dungeon's **Compass**.

Leave this room, go right, then hit the crystal, go down, then hit the crystal here to open up the path to the right.

Top Tip!

You can stand on top of a colored block that's in the ground while hitting the crystal. Doing so causes Link to raise up with the block. This can used to make it easier to both dodge enemies and hit other crystals sooner than intended!

In this room, jump across the lowered orange blocks, collecting the floating powder top-up, and then jump across onto the switch beside the blue crystal. A chest appears above you, so jump across and open it for a **Small Key**. Jump back across to the lowered orange blocks, then proceed North into the next room.

Use a charged spinning attack on the two Shy Guys simultaneously to reveal a **Small Key**. It's safe to leave this room now, so head back down, jump across the gaps, head left, then hit the switch before going up, then go right, and collect the **Small Key**.

Go left again and hit the crystals to reach the side of the room where the two Shy Guys were. Now go right and use your shield to flip the **Spiked Beetles** in this room. Open up the locked door and proceed to the next room.

Dispose of the two Keese in here (while also watching out for the **Spark** making its way around the room).

Push the left-hand wooden block right so it slides onto the right stone and push the right-hand wooden block right, so it slides onto the left stone. Doing so reveals a stairwell to a 2D platforming section.

Jump across the gaps and moving platforms and you'll reappear in a dark room. Ignore the unlit torches, for now, and proceed North and you'll reappear in the mini-boss room.

Mini-Boss: Hinox

This mini-boss' main method of attack is to follow you around the room and then try and grab you with its big arms. You need to be very careful of the cracked tiles on the outer-edges of the room, as standing on them for too long will cause them to crumble (making it harder to move around the room safely).

The trick here is to constantly jump around the room in either a clockwise or an anti-clockwise direction. Constantly jumping prevents you from standing on a cracked floor tile for too long and going in a circular direction will buy you time as it tries to grab you.

Once the creature misses, quickly attack it from the side to get a hit in (it'll flash red when you are successful). It takes a total of six hits to beat this mini-boss.

Grab the **Fairy**, if needed, and then in the next room, go up, and jump across the gaps here towards the Owl statue. Jump across the next gap and enter the door here.

This room has a few Keese in it along with a new enemy type, the **Vacuum Mouth**. For a few seconds, this purple ball sucks everything towards it.

So, you need to keep pressing in the opposite direction (while still moving up towards the chest). Open the chest to receive the **Map**. Head down and right and then make your way up to the door at the top of the room.

The chest here holds a **Red Rupee** for **20 rupees**. Now open the locked door and the next room has two very familiar enemies (at least, if you've played a Mario game before).

Two **Boos** begin chasing you. Quickly jump upwards and then to the left. Head towards the unlit torch and use your magic powder to light it. This makes the Boos vulnerable to your sword. Attack them both and once they're finished, a chest will appear. Open it to receive the, very handy, **Power Bracelet**!

The Power Bracelet allows you to pick up heavier objects (which, for the moment at least, means pots and light grey rocks). Also, they're equipped automatically for you, so you never need to worry about that. Sweet!

Head back into the previous room and start lifting up the pots at the top of the room. Proceed right, towards the *orange* floor tiles, but attack the *blue* crystal while standing on the edge of the last *orange* tile.

This causes the orange tiles to rise. Jump across the gap to the other *orange* tiles, and then turn back around to hit the orange crystal. This causes the *orange* tiles to drop, granting you access to the chest. Open it up to obtain a **Small Key**.

Walk back to the crystal, hit it to raise the *orange* tiles, but walk right (so the *blue* tiles are now lowered, opening the way). Proceed right, but take care of the **Hardhat Beetle**, **Keese**, and the **Yellow Stalfos** blocking your path.

You want to go to the open doorway at the bottom of this room. *You must dispose of the enemies here in the correct order for the chest to appear!*

So, follow these steps in this order to succeed:
1. Push the right-hand wooden block down one space.
2. Push the left-hand block left one space.
3. You can either head up, collect a pot, and throw the pot at the **Pols Voice** that's hopping around. Or, you can get up close and use your Magic Powder on it to get rid of it. Your choice.
4. Take out the **Keese** bat next.

5. Finally, use your shield to block the **Shrouded Stalfos'** spears *before* counter-attacking with your sword.

Removing the enemies in this order causes a chest to appear. Open it to obtain the **Nightmare Key** for this dungeon. Nice.

Go up, open the locked door on the right and use a pot, or your powder, on the Pols Voice hopping around in front of you. Disposing of both Pols Voice enemies causes some steps to appear. Head down them to appear in a new side-scrolling section.

Stand on the stone platform to make it slowly sink to the lower floor. Now go left, pick up the pot in front of you, and then climb the ladder while holding it (don't ask me how Link's managing to climb a ladder with no hands – but he can!). Now, stand on top of the next gray platform with the pot over your head and it'll slowly start to sink. Climb the ladder to reach the next room.

Walk down to the center of the room and then jump across the gaps until you reach the door to the boss' room!

Nightmare Boss Fight

Phase 1: Breaking the Bottle

The tick to beating this boss is to break his bottle (making him vulnerable to your sword). To achieve this, begin the fight by standing right in front of the boss and hold up your shield.

The fireballs won't hurt you.

Once the Genie is done throwing the fireballs, run up to the bottle and strike it to knock it over. Now pick the bottle up, run up to the wall in front of you, and then throw the bottle at it. This causes the bottle to crack.

Now repeat this pattern of dodging the fireballs, striking the bottle, and throwing it at the wall two more times to finally break the bottle for good.

Phase 2: Attacking the Genie

Immediately make your way into the middle of the room and let the two ghosts of the Genie circle around you. When they stop, wait for the Genie to throw the large fireball towards you.

Hug the left-hand wall to dodge the fireball, then get in close to the Genie and start attacking it with your sword. After a couple of hits, it'll split back into two more ghosts again.

So, once again, stand in the middle of the room and wait for it to form back into the real Genie. Wait for it to throw the fireball at you, run around it, and then get in a couple more hits to finish it off for good!

Your rewards are a **Heart Container** and, in the next room, the **Conch Horn**!

Top Tip! Immediately after exiting the dungeon, go right back in, throw away the pots, and open the chest here for a helpful **Purple Rupee** worth **50 rupees**!

Chapter 6

The Journey to the third dungeon

Taking BowWow Back Home

Once you've left the second dungeon again, stick to the top of the screen and attack the flowers and enemies so BowWow can eat them. Go down and then left to the screen with the telephone booth hut, then jump up and across the gap here. Walk into the cave in front of you, lift the skull in front of the chest, and open the chest for a **Purple Rupee** worth **50 rupees**.

Now head left and jump across the gap to another chest. Open it for a **Red Rupee** worth **20 rupees**. Exit the cave, dispose of the Moblins and other enemies and keep going South. Stick to the left side of the Mysterious Forest, grabbing the **Mushroom** along the way, and then enter the cave via the tree stump.

You can now grab the Heart Piece that's here. So, push the lower-tight rock right, go up, push the block to your left further left, go up, push the next rock up against the wall, then lift the two skulls to claim your **Heart Piece**.

Heart Piece 03/32

Pushing stone puzzle, tree stump cave.

(Mysterious Forest)

Collected?

Now go right, push the farthest right block one square right, then the rock above you towards the wall. Proceed into the next room and exit the cave.

Magic Powder Upgrade

Immediately proceed North, get rid of the Moblin, and then pick up the rock to your right to reveal a set of steps leading underground. Approach the unlit torch and throw some Magic Powder on it. Doing so causes it to burst into life. A large purple bat will threaten you with the ability to carry more Magic Powder! Oh no! What a terrible fate! Once you agree to this terrible burden, Link will now be able to carry a total of **40 magic powder sprinkles**. Sweet!

Exit the cave, go South, then left through the narrow gap, and look for a rock just South of your location. Lift up the rock and open the chest here for your first **Secret Seashell**! Hmm... I wonder what these are for?

Secret Seashell 01/50
Inside a chest, close to Mabe Village.

(Mysterious Forest)

Collected?

Make your way back to **Mabe Village** and head into Madam MeowMeow's house to return BowWow to her. After she gives Link a huge smooch on the cheeks as a thank-you, go back outside and then go right and make your way inside the Trendy Game store (it has the blue and red tiles on the roof).

Mini-Game: Trendy Game

This mini-game requires you to guide a mechanical arm over the top of an item that you want to collect. You can only move the arm up or right (leaving you less room for error). You use the **X** button to move the crane arm forward and the **A** button to move the crane arm right.

To begin the mini-game, approach the man behind the counter and give him **10 rupees** to play. Now approach the two purple buttons to gain control of the crane arm. Once you start playing, you can stay at the controls and just pay another 10 rupees to play again. You can keep playing until you have less than 10 rupees left.

Trading Side-Quest Item 1: Yoshi Doll

The first item to collect is the **Yoshi Doll**. A top tip here is to look for the light shining down from the crane onto the floor below.

If the light is directly over the top of the item you want, you know it's a guarantee you'll grab it. So, press the right button until the crane is in front of you, then push the up button once to grab the **Yoshi Doll**.

Swing the crane right and let go of the button just as the crane passes over the dark rectangle on the floor. The crane should now stop in front of the Heart Piece. Take the crane arm up one square and stop. If you've been following this guide, then collecting this **Heart Piece** will earn you another full heart container. Nice!

Heart Piece 04/32

Collect it with the claw, Trendy Game.

(Mabe Village)

Collected?

Mabe Village Item Bonanza

Exit the Trendy Game hut and proceed North (past the wind vane). Go up the steps and then enter the house on the left with the green roof. Walk up to the mother carrying the crying baby and she'll give you the **Ribbon** in return for the Yoshi Doll.

Now head South and enter the side-house that's attached to Madam MoewMoew's house. Speak to **CiaoCiao** inside and she'll trade you some **Canned Food** for the Ribbon.

Head back outside and then go right. Look for the square patch of bushes that's surrounded by grass. Cut your way through the bushes on the second-from-top row and you'll uncover a **Secret Seashell** tucked away.

Secret Seashell 02/50

Inside the bushes, above Trendy Game.

(Mabe Village)

Collected?

Before you go any further, make sure you have at least **210** rupees (which you will do if you've been following our guide closely). Now head straight up and enter the **Town Tool Shop**. Pick up the **Deluxe Shovel** and take it to the shop keeper where he'll deduct 200 rupees for buying it. Now pick up the pack of **10 Bombs** and pay for those too.

Note

The Yoshi Doll is the first item in a side-quest where you need to find someone to give the item to. They will then swap it for a different item (that someone else wants). You'll eventually, earn an *essential* item for completing this side-quest.

Head outside, go into the menu, and then equip the Deluxe Shovel to a button. Go back to CiaoCiao's room and use your shovel in the bottom right-hand corner of the room to reveal the next **Secret Seashell**!

Secret Seashell 03/50

Bottom right-hand corner, CiaoCiao's room.

(Mabe Village)

Collected?

To Kanalet Castle

Go South to **Toronbo Shores** and keep traveling right until you reach the small hut with the giant flower on its roof. Go inside and trade the Canned Food in return for some **Bananas**.

33

Leave the hut, head left, and go back to **Mabe Village**. When you get there, go back to where the shop is but, this time, keep going right. Pick up the rocks in your way and you'll enter the new area known as **Ukuku Prairie**. As soon as you do, go North and into the cave's entrance.

To reach both the chest and the **Heart Piece** in this room, you need to push the rocks in the right direction and in the correct order (but watch out for the enemies that will get in your way):

1. Push the top-left rock upwards and quickly run past the cracked floor panel.

2. Now push the rock to your right one square to the right.

3. Lift up the skull and you'll see five rocks in a "V" shape. Push the rock located at the top-right tip of this "V" to the right (so it hits the wall and is above the skull).

4. Push the rock that's beside the skull down towards the wall.

5. Lift up the skull and then collect the **Heart Piece**.

6. Push the rock that's in front of the chest to the left and open the chest to obtain a **Purple Rupee** worth **50 rupees**.

Heart Piece 05/32

Rock pushing puzzle, inside a cave.

(Ukuku Prairie)

Collected?

Go back outside, climb the nearby ladder, and lift the rock out of the way to reach **Koholint Prairie**. Go right and head straight into the **Cemetery**. You should see four gravestones down below you. Get in front of the bottom-right gravestone and push it forwards to reveal a stairwell underground.

Push the rock, located to your right, one square right and get rid of the Keese with your sword. Now it's time for a tricky jump. Aim Link towards the top-left corner of the platform below you and then jump at an angle from the rock you just pushed.

If you time it just right, Link will make it onto the platform, allowing you to jump up and collect the **Heart Piece**. You only need to push the rock away to your left to get back out. Phew!

Heart Piece 06/32

Tricky platform jump.

(Cemetery)

Collected?

Go back into the Cemetery and then retrace your steps so you go back down the ladder to Ukuku Prairie. Go further South and touch the flat stone slab with blue swirls to trigger your first fast travel/warp point in the game. Now travel South and go into the tall grass in between the wall and the next dungeon where you'll arrive in **Pothole Field**.

Keep walking South until you see a small hut with some grass on top of it. Enter it and speak to the blue-haired boy known as **Richard**. He'll begin a new side-quest where he asks you to retrieve **Five Golden Leaves**.

Leave his home, go right, and then up through **Ukuku Prairie**. Take the first right, dodge the Zirro, and then head North. Take the path heading right at the tree with the rotary telephone on top, go down at the next junction, then head right until you see the group of Boarblins.

Clear the Boarblins out go up towards the Seashell hut but go right. Cut down the top-right corner bush to reveal the next **Secret Seashell**.

Secret Seashell 04/50

In a bush, right-side of Secret Seashell hut.

(Ukuku Prairie)

Collected?

35

Now look for the dark swirl in the patch of dirt to your left. Use your shovel on the swirl to create a link to the warp point you activated a few minutes ago.

Now drop down from the ledge go right, and then up the path beside the Zorro-infested water. At the top, speak with **Kiki the Monkey** who will trade your Bananas for a newly built bridge and a dropped **Stick**. Sounds fair enough to us!

Kanalet Castle and the Five Golden Leaves

Go over the wooden bridge, keep walking North, and then turn left at the apple tree. Cut the bush beside it to reveal some steps heading underground.

You can either drop down on top of the Goomba's head or attack them with your sword. Now jump across the spike-filled gaps, then jump up and climb the ladder into the Castle's grounds.

Defeat the **Mad Bomber** that pops up out of the four holes to earn the first **Golden Leaf**.

Make your way down to the bottom wall of the castle, take out the two **Darknuts**, then continue to the far left-hand side. Go up and look for the **Crow** resting on top of the tree.

Pick up a nearby rock and throw it at the tree to scare the crow. Once it comes to attack you, hit it with your sword and once it's gone, you can collect the next **Golden Leaf**.

Make your way back to the Castle's main entrance and head inside and dodge the fiery **Bubble** enemy that bounces from surface-to-surface.

Get rid of the two **Darknuts** and the **Gel**. The next **Golden Leaf** then drops down from the sky.

Continue North, then proceed to get rid of the two Darknuts. Continue East and dispose of the Darknut and the Keese. Now step on the button to open up the main gates to the castle. Now use the steps to reach the next floor of the castle.

Walk down into the area with the two lit torches. Equip your bombs and use one on the left-hand cracked Darknut statue. This causes the first Darknut to become free and it attacks you. Once you've gotten rid of it, you can now collect the next **Golden Leaf**.

Go back up the steps, head right, then down, and go outside. Go inside the castle again, lift a pot, and then throw it at the locked down to smash it open. However, make sure you're at full health *before* you enter the door as the next enemy can be quite tough. You can smash some more of the pots to find extra small hearts.

This enemy requires a total of **10** sword attacks to get rid of. We recommend that you jump around the edges of the room, making it easier to dodge its spiked-ball attacks. Once you see its spike-ball get stuck in the wall, immediately jump to the soldier, and then get in as many sword attacks as you can. Simply repeat this process until it gives up the ghost and reveals the, fifth and final, **Golden Leaf**.

Side-Quest Rewards and the Dungeon Key

With all five Golden Leaves in hand, head back outside, leave the castle, and proceed South back through **Pothole Field** and make your way back to Richard's house.

Push the statue right, walk down the stairs, take the left-hand path, push the rock into the whole, jump across, and claim the **Secret Seashell** from the chest.

Secret Seashell 05/50

Underneath Richard's home.

(Pothole Field)

Collected? ☐

Now go right, up, climb the stairs, and then head down the steps that lead outside. You'll reappear in a bush-laden area. Before moving, understand that this is effectively a puzzle as many bushes conceal a pothole that will sap you of half a heart every time you fall into one. However, once you reach the end, you'll be rewarded with the next **Heart Piece** for your efforts.

Heart Piece 07/32

Top of Pothole Field, Richard's reward.

(Pothole Field)

Collected? ☐

Jump back across the gap from the heart piece and then cut down the bushes in the following order: Down two, left three, up one, and left. Get out your **Shovel**, cut the bush in front of the Owl, and then dig the ground where the bush was. You'll reveal the **Slime Key** that opens up the next dungeon! Sweet!

Pick up the nearby rock, throw it away, and then jump across the gap for a shortcut to the dungeon's keyhole. Use the key and the dungeon's bars will drop. However, you still need to make it to the entrance.

To do this, go back down the steps, continue down past Richard's hut, go right, then up, and at the next junction, go up the small hill to your left. Go down the path beside the water, jump across to each platform to the other side, head up the stairs, then take out the two Winged Octorocks that attack you.

While you're up here, dig the ground on the left (near the ledge), to reveal a **Secret Seashell**!

Secret Seashell 06/50

Dig the ground above the Slime dungeon.

(Ukuku Prairie)

Collected? ☐

38

Third Dungeon: Key Cavern

Use a pot on the locked door to bust it wide open. In the next room, watch out for the **Bombite** enemies. Attacking them with your sword causes them to bounce around the room and then explode (taking out anyone in the blast radius). Make sure every enemy is disposed of to reveal a chest with a **Small Key** inside.

Go into the open door in front of the chest and take out the four Gels. When the chest appears, open it, but immediately begin swiping your sword. It's a trap! A Gel appears, so get rid of it and you'll often be rewarded with a Piece of Power for your troubles. Now go up, continue North into the next room, and then head down the steps.

Use the small key on the locked door at the top of the room, dispose of the enemies in here, hit the crystal (to turn it orange), and then collect the **Small Key** before leaving. Go back up the stairs and then open up the chest to reveal the **Stone Beak** for this dungeon.

Continue South, past the two Stalfos', and then at the booby-trapped chest, take the right-hand door. Get rid of the enemies and then open up the chest for this dungeon's **Map**.

Leave this room, head up, and then go straight down the steps. Open up the right-hand door and you'll see a conveyor belt with a **Pairodd** enemy on it. Feel free to ignore it as you jump across the conveyor belts and then head up the steps.

In this room, go into each upper corner to reveal some Gel enemies. They all need to be taken care of and a **Small Key** will then drop to the floor. Collect it and then head North.

Go up to the top-right corner of the next room and then head right. Dispose of the enemies in here and the door beside the broken Owl statue will open.

When you attack any of the Bombites in here, you trigger a 3-second countdown until they explode. Let them get close until you see their counter reach 1. Now push them away from you with your sword to minimize the risk of damage. The door only opens once every enemy is gone.

There's a well-hidden secret in this room. Plant a bomb by the wall that's directly opposite the door. While the fuse is burning down, open up the chest for the **Compass**. Dispose of the Bombites in here to reveal a **Small Key**.

Walk back to the broken Owl statue and you'll notice the **blue** tiles make an arrow shape. Bomb the Southern wall (at the tip of the "arrow") to open up access to another room.

Clear this room of enemies and then bomb the cracked part of the left-hand wall. Continue left, disposing of the Gels, and when the doors open up, go inside the left-hand door.

Throw your bombs at the two **Pairodds** and clear the room of the Gels. Using the bombs prevents the Pairodds from jumping around the room as they'll stand still while you hit them with your bombs. Collect the **Small Key** that drops from the roof.

Head North and then clear the next room of all enemies. Doing so causes a chest to appear on a higher-level to your right. We'll collect that soon enough, so don't worry. Proceed North into the next room.

There's a hovering cache of 10 Bombs to collect (usually a good indication that you'll need to use them for an upcoming battle or puzzle), so jump to collect them and dispose of the enemies before climbing the steps to the next level of the dungeon.

First head down and open the chest for a **Purple Rupee** worth **50 rupees**. Keep going South and push the wooden block away at the bottom of the steps. Go up into the nearby open door and be ready to use the extra bombs you collected a minute ago.

Top Tip!

Picking up a lit bomb deactivates the bomb's fuse, allowing you to replace, or throw, the bomb without worrying about it exploding on your head after you pick it up!

Mini-Boss: Dodongo Snakes

These two mini-bosses randomly crawl around the small room. The trick here is that you must throw a bomb into their mouths as they open them. They won't eat them off the ground. So, you must time your throws so that the bomb reaches their mouth as they're opening (which means standing in front of them).

Remember, if you mistime a throw, picking up the bomb causes the fuse to stop burning (prevents you wasting bombs). Each black mini-boss requires three bombs to dispose of.

Once they're both gone, head right, push the lower wooden block left, and then the block beside it up. Open the chest to reveal the classic **Pegasus Boots**!

Pegasus Boots

The Pegasus Boots are auto-equipped, which allows you to dash through those large black crystals, or simply run across large open spaces very quickly.

So, dash through the two large crystals in your way, push the wooden block right, and then head down. Now for some cool moves.

In this room, stand inside the blown-up bit of wall on the right and then dash towards the large open pit. Press jump just before you reach the pit, and the extra speed allows Link to leap much further than normal. Repeat this step to reach the chest and open it for this dungeon's **Nightmare Key**!

Jump off the ledge to your left, go left, then down, and head back to the warp-portal in the mini-boss' room. From the entrance, go right, and then line yourself up in front of the **Vacuum Mouth**. Dash towards it (being careful not to get pushed into the pit below). Open up the chest for a **Small Key**.

Go back to the entrance, then head up, then left, and dash up, through the two black crystals. Go up one more screen and get rid of the **Gel**. Now, come back down two more screens, and head up into the door on the right. Dispose of the two Stalfos to make a chest appear. Inside you'll find your first **Golden Rupee** worth a wallet-bursting **300 rupees**! Amazing!

Now go back to the main entrance and take the warp portal. Go South into the main large room and start using your small keys on the metal lock-covered blocks. With the fourth locked block gone, head down the steps.

Dash into the **Mega Thwomp** to make it drop down, now dash right, jump right, and hold **UP** on the controller as you reach the ladder to grab it and avoid the spikes below. Clear out the Piranha Plant from the pipe, then go down the ladder.

Use your dash attack to clear the room of **Pairodds**. In the next room, get rid of all of the Keese and collect the **Small Key** that drops down. Now open the door to begin the boss battle.

Nightmare Boss Fight

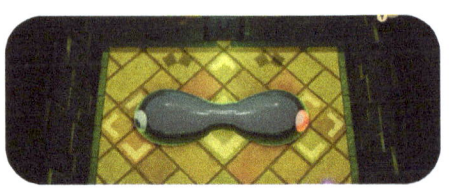

Slime Eye

The boss thinks it's being clever by hiding from you. Show it who's the real boss by dashing against any wall to make it drop down from the roof.

Begin by hitting the boss with your sword to force it to begin splitting apart. Once there's a stretch in the middle, hit one of the eyes two more times to stun it long enough for you to dash through the middle of the boss, splitting it into two separate enemies.

Each eye now requires **four** direct attacks to get rid of them for good. Just be wary of the fact that they both like to jump up high and track your movements around the room.

You can see exactly where they are by their shadows on the ground. Make sure to jump out of the way (as the dash takes a second to charge up, leaving you defenseless).

Once both parts are gone, collect the **Heart Container** and then go up to collect the next instrument, the **Sea Lily's Bell**.

Chapter 7

The Journey to the fourth dungeon

To the Dream Shrine

From the entrance of the third dungeon, proceed right, and jump across the water using the platforms. Go up, then right, then climb up the ladder, walk down the nearby steps, and drop a bomb by the cracked pig skull statue.

Now go North and speak with **Tarin** who's standing in front of a beehive. He'll ask to borrow your **Stick** for a – not very wise – plan. Once Tarin has ran away, pick up the **Honeycomb** to keep on top of this trading sub-quest.

Immediately above you is a wall with an off-colored breakable bit of wall. Plan a bomb there, go inside, and speak to the **Great Fairy** to have all of your energy replenished – for free! And you can visit her as often as you like (you'll also find a Fairy or two flying around that you can use if needed).

Leave the room and follow this wall around to your left (through the bushes and the grass). You'll soon reach a tree beside another breakable wall. So, blow it up, head inside, and dodge the Spark as you dash through the black crystals.

Make your way around the rocks but, before opening the chest below, go up and there's a cracked part in the right-hand wall. Blow it up to reveal the next **Heart Piece**!

Heart Piece 08/32

Hidden cave room, West of Honeycomb.

(Ukuku Prairie)

Collected?

Go back out, dash down, and then open the chest for a **Purple Rupee**. Make your way back around the room to the exit and proceed back into **Ukuku Prairie**.

Go South and walk near the warp point. Continue walking past it to the left and look for a tree that's standing to the right of the hut with the telephone on top. Dash into this tree to reveal a well-hidden **Secret Seashell**!

Secret Seashell 07/50

Dash into a tree near the telephone hut.

(Ukuku Prairie)

Collected?

Turn around, go North, and the lift the rocks on your left that are blocking your access to **Mabe Village**. Go up to the top, the left, and lift up one of the rocks blocking access to the stone house. Inside, you'll enter the **Dream Shine**. Go up the steps and rest in the bed to reappear in a new area.

Top Tip!

Keep an eye out for trees with either Green or Red apples on them. If you dash in to a tree, the apple drops down. Pick it up to restore some health. Green apples restore three hearts, while Red apples restore one heart. You can also store an apple in an empty jar!

To the Color Dungeon

You'll encounter a new enemy here known as an **Arm Mimic**. These can be disposed of using regular sword attacks. But, because they mimic your direction of movement, dashing into them is a far more effective way to deal with them.

Stop dashing when you see the first set of steps, head up, and open the chest for your first **Silver Rupee** that's worth a cool **100 rupees!** Go down, dash through the black crystal, and then head up to collect the Ocarina!

Ocarina

Your tool of choice for quickly using those Warp Zones that are dotted all around Koholint Island. There's also a total of three different tunes Link can learn as his adventure progresses.

Once collected, go down the steps, and drop off of the ledge on the left, leave the dream house, and now go speak with **Marin** who's standing by the weather-vane. After speaking with her, you'll learn the **Ballad of the Wind Fish**.

Now go towards where the two boys are playing in the village and enter the **Library** beside them. Dash into the bookshelf at the back of the Library and read the book that drops down.

The book tells you how to access the special color dungeon (that was added to the color-enhanced DX release of the game for the Gameboy Color back in December 1998).

Now make your way back through the village and head to **Ukuku Prairie**. Climb the nearby ladder (that has the rock at the top), then go up, and to the right into the **Cemetery**. The five gravestones can be found in the bottom right-hand corner.

Push the gravestones in the correct direction. For convenience, we've added a screenshot that shows you the correct order in which to push each of the gravestones. Just be very careful of the ghosts that appear from each gravestone as you push them, they can be a pain to get rid of.

The Color Dungeon

Approach the red and blue dungeon keepers and they'll warn you that you'll need some **Magic Powder** to make it through this special dungeon. Good job we have some then, isn't it!

Head up to the first room and quickly dodge the red and green **Camo Goblins** that slide around the floor before popping up to attack you. Cut them down to size and then go through the next door.

To solve this particular puzzle, you must hit the sphere until all four spheres match the same color. Firstly, to turn them all blue, hit the top-left sphere first, then hit the bottom right-hand sphere. This causes a chest to appear, which contains the dungeon's **Compass**. You should now bomb the cracked Southern wall. Step through for a veritable goldmine of Blue **Rupees**. Nice!

In the next room, the colored tiles are all weak. Every time you stand on one, it'll change color. Green tiles can take three steps, yellow tiles can take two more steps before they drop, red tiles only one more step. Use the pot to get rid of the flying **Shrouded Stalfos**. Now jump across the tiles to the opening on the right.

In this room, attack each of the colored **Orb Monsters**, then pick it up once it turns into a ball and throw it into the same-colored hole. A chest will appear containing this dungeon's **Stone Beak**.

In the adjoining room, jump across the tiles as fast as possible into the next room. In here you come across four more colored spheres. To turn them all blue, hit the bottom right-hand sphere first, then the top left-hand sphere twice. A **Small Key** drops down in return.

Proceed right into the next room, clear it out (or just unlock the door with your small key). However, you'll want to equip your **Magic Powder** *before* entering this next room, as it leads to a mini-boss fight!

Mini-Boss: Giant Buzz Blob

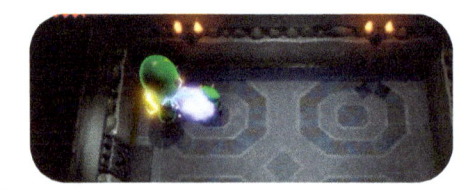

46

This enemy is only vulnerable to your sword when it's a **blue** blob. As soon as it turns **green** (and becomes electrifying), use your magic powder on it to turn it back into that vulnerable **blue** blob again. Now attack it as often as you can (while dodging it as it jumps at you). Keep this up until it's gone for good.

In the next room, push the top and bottom blocks left one space and the middle block up one. Now open the chest to claim this dungeon's **Nightmare Key**.

Now make your way back to the room with the **red** and **blue** Orb Monsters and go through the Southern door. Clear the room of enemies and the left-hand door will open up again.

In the next room, wait for the Shrouded Stalfos' to get closer before attacking (due to the tiled floor ahead). Jump across the tiles and open the chest for a **Small Key**. Now head North into the next room.

Use the pot on the Flying Stalfos to knock it down and then hop across the tiles to the locked door opposite. Open the door and proceed through it.

Mini-Boss: Avalaunch

This mini-boss jumps on the ground causing three rocks to drop from the ceiling. These rocks then bounce around the room, doing plenty of damage. If you have sufficient bombs to hand, stand opposite the enemy and throw a bomb into the middle of the room. The blast radius will more than likely connect and hurt the mini-boss. **Six bombs** will do the trick.

> **Top Tip!**
> The upcoming mini-boss fight becomes much easier if you have at least eight bombs to hand. If not, try your best to get some from fallen enemies in the surrounding rooms.

Alternatively, the more frustrating strategy is to get closer to the boss and to do jumping charged sword attacks. You want to time your jumps so that Link is in the air when the enemy lands on the ground. Otherwise, Link will fall down, leaving him much more vulnerable to getting hit by the rocks (which become very annoying, very quickly).

In the next room, quickly jump across the tiles before the leaping Shrouded Stalfos' break all of the tiles for you! Now lift up the pot at the top of the room, step on the hidden switch, and enter the Northern door.

Clear this room of enemies and open the chest that appears for the dungeon's **Map**. In the next room, simply get the Orb Monsters into their appropriately colored holes in the floor. You can do this by hitting them there with your sword, or picking them up and throwing them in. Collect the **Small Key** that appears.

Go back through the last room and then take the left-hand door in the room with the jumping Shrouded Stalfos'. Time for another colored sphere puzzle!

To turn all of these spheres blue, strike the top-middle sphere, then the middle sphere on the far-left, then the middle sphere at the bottom, and finally the middle sphere on the far-right.

Enter the top door, clear the room of Gels, smash open the pots for any goodies inside, and then in the next room, stand on the blue tile and hit the crystal, lowering the orange tiles that prevented access to the boss' door.

Boss: Hardhit Beetle

Hardhit Beetle

To be honest, the best strategy here is to be very aggressive from the start and keep getting up close to the boss while attacking it with your sword. Don't let up and after nine hits, it'll be done for. If you've been following our guide up to now, then you'll have more than enough hearts to tank the hits.

48

In the next room, you'll speak with the **Fairy Queen**. As a reward for finishing this dungeon, you can choose from only one of two rewards:

1. **Red** Mail: Permanently doubles your sword's attack power.

2. **Blue** Mail: Permanently halves the amount of damage Link takes when hit.

Our suggestion on which one to choose is to select the **Red** Mail if you're playing on the default difficulty level (as Link takes less damage on this difficulty as standard).

On the harder difficulty level (unlocked after beating the game once), selecting the **Blue** Mail is definitely a wise choice as Link takes more damage.

Item Collect-a-thon

With your shiny new Red Mail in tow, go North out of the **Cemetery** and equip your **Shovel**. Enter the **Tabahl Wasteland** and stick to the right-hand side. Look for a pothole near a tree, just down and to the right of this pothole is a patch of dirt. Shovel it to find the next **Secret Seashell**!

Secret Seashell 08/50
Dig the patch of dirt near the top-right.

(Tabahl Wasteland)

Collected?

And no sooner have we collected another seashell, but it's time to pick up a cheekily hidden **Heart Piece** nearby!

Heart Piece 09/32
Behind the trees at the top of the field.

(Tabahl Wasteland)

Collected?

Immediately travel down to the South-Western corner of the Wasteland and go back to **Koholint Prairie**. Start running down until you reach the rock that blocks the ladder. Lift the rock, go down the ladder and you're now back in **Ukuku Prairie**.

Proceed East, past where you collected the Honeycomb from the tree, go up the steps and then down the ladder, now go North, then East at the telephone hut, then South at the junction, enter into the rocky area with the **Boarblins** and **Zirros**. Pick up the boulder for a **Secret Seashell**.

Secret Seashell 09/50
Under a rock, middle of the boulder maze.

(Ukuku Prairie)

Collected?

Go up and leave the rocky area and look right for a Zirro flying near a wooden signpost. Keep walking right until you see a single bush at the end of three trees. Cut the bush down to reveal a hidden set of steps. Go down these steps.

Watch out for the Piranha fish and then dash through the black crystals to the steps leading up.

Immediately dash South and you'll arrive in **Martha's Bay**. Dash across to the far-right of the screen and you'll see a house over on the right, in **Animal Village**. Enter it and give **Chef Bear** the **Honeycomb**. In return, he'll give you a **Pineapple**.

Upon leaving Chef's house, go South and activate the next Warp Tile. Keep standing on the tile to bring up the Warp Screen. Warp to **Ukuku Prairie**. Go left and enter **Mabe Village**. Head into the **Town Tool Shop** and stock up on some more bombs.

Now head South towards the entrance to the first dungeon. It's time to collect another hidden **Secret Seashell**!

Secret Seashell 10/50

Dash into the lonely tree, near 1st dungeon.

(Tail Cave Entrance)

Collected?

Now proceed back inside the first dungeon again. Now go up one screen, left one screen, up one screen, and then look for the cracked wall on the left-side. Blow this up, enter the room, and open the chest for *another* **Secret Seashell**!

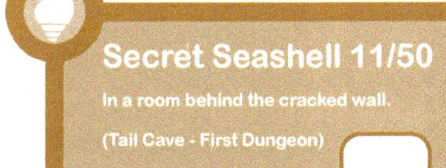

Secret Seashell 11/50

In a room behind the cracked wall.

(Tail Cave - First Dungeon)

Collected?

51

Exit the dungeon once again, make your way back onto the nearby **Toronbo Shores**, stick to the far-left side of the beach and look for the Octorock moving around four trees. Dash into the bottom-right tree to reveal the next **Secret Seashell**.

Secret Seashell 12/50

Dash into bottom-right palm tree.

(Toronbo Shores)

Collected?

Now start dashing across the crisp sand to the far-right side of the beach. Look for a chest blocked by some rocks. Lift the rocks, open the chest, and pocket the **Purple Rupee**. Immediately after, head South and speak to **Marin** by the log.

Once Marin has agreed to join you, don't run away. Instead, walk around the tree to your left and dig up the sand in the far-left corner to reveal *another* **Secret Seashell**.

Secret Seashell 13/50

Dig the sand left of where you meet Marin.

(Toronbo Shores)

Collected?

Open the Path to Yarna Desert

In an effort to get that "good" 100% ending, take Marin to the very far left side of the beach. Once you reach the left-hand barrier, go down until you trigger a cut-scene.

Head North to **Mabe Village** and then proceed East to the **Ukuku Prairie Warp Point**. Warp back to **Animal Village**.

Go up, then left past the trees, then down, and finally right. You should spot the big sleeping walrus blocking your path. It's time to enter the next new area!

Retrieving the Fourth Dungeon Key

Go right, then go up and dash up to the top where the sand is moving into the center. A large mini-boss known as **Lanmola** will start leaping through the sand.

You must hit its head with your sword while staying away from the center of the screen as the sand will suck you under, causing you to drop into a cave that you need to head right (and then climb the steps) to get out of.

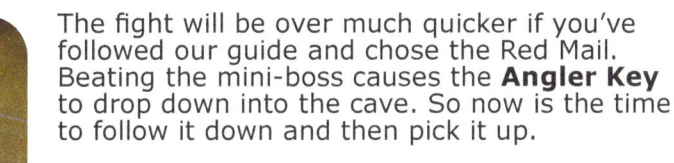

The fight will be over much quicker if you've followed our guide and chose the Red Mail. Beating the mini-boss causes the **Angler Key** to drop down into the cave. So now is the time to follow it down and then pick it up.

After collecting the key, bomb the cracked Northern wall to reveal a hidden room. Make sure to collect the **Heart Piece** found inside.

Heart Piece 10/32

Behind a cracked wall, Angler Key Cave.

(Yarna Desert)

Collected?

Now exit the cave by using the steps and you reappear back in the desert. Watch out for the spiny **Orange Leever** enemies here (as well as the **Pokeys** that look like cacti). Immediately stick to the right-hand side of the screen and dash down the narrow path to the bottom right-hand corner of the desert. Now pick up the bottom rock here to reveal the next **Secret Seashell**.

Secret Seashell 14/50

Under a rock, bottom right-hand corner.

(Yarna Desert)

Collected?

53

It's now time to make your way back to the desert's entrance (where you met the Walrus). Once you get there, take out your Ocarina and play **Marin's tune**, and the Walrus appears. As a thank-you, the Walrus throws you up a **Secret Seashell**.

Secret Seashell 15/50
Thank-you gift from the Walrus.

(Yarna Desert)

Collected?

Opening the Fourth Dungeon

Now immediately proceed North so you're on the right-hand side of the wooden posts by **Animal Village**. Dash around the side, and then the top, of the village to reach a hidden **Heart Piece**.

Heart Piece 11/32
End of a path between village and desert.

(Animal Village)

Collected?

Run back down to the **Warp Tile** in Animal Village and warp to **Ukuku Prairie**. Now go up, climb up the ladder with the rock at the top, keep going up (lifting the rocks in your way), go left (towards the entrance to the Prairie), then up to **Tal Tal Heights** (near the swamp's dungeon entrance).

Go up and then take a right up the hill where all the **Moblins** are roaming around. Look for a wooden signpost that's in between three rocks. Lift up the right-hand rock to reveal a **Secret Seashell**.

Secret Seashell 16/50
Under a rock, beside wooden sign-post.

(Tal Tal Heights)

Collected?

Now go right and look for a rock sitting in the middle of the grass. Lift it up to reveal a warp zone for **Dampé's Shack**. Go back to where you found the last Secret Seashell, lift the two rocks, run up the slope, dash to the far right, lift the rock blocking the path, and head down the ladder.

Watch out for the **Lue Tektites** that jump around down here. Stand in front of the waterfall and use the **Angler Key** to open up the entrance to the next dungeon. Equip your bombs and look for the nearby hole that's behind you. Throw a bomb into the hole (you'll find out why soon enough).

Proceed to the **Warp Tile**, activate it, and throw a bomb down the hole to the right of the warp tile. Wait a few second for it to explode and it'll throw up a **Secret Seashell** for you! Nice!

Secret Seashell 17/50

Throw a bomb in the hole by the warp tile.

(Tal Tal Heights)

Collected?

To the Fourth Dungeon

Now make your way left, past the dungeon's keyhole, up the ladder, and then climb the Northern ladder that leads you into the dusty **Tal Tal Mountain Range**.

Lift the rocks outside the cave, head inside, jump across the gap to the top of the room, head right, quickly dash across the cracked tiles, and push the rock down, opening up the pathway.

After heading down the steps, immediately go back up them. This resets the rocks in the previous room. Push the rock South of you down one, and then push the left-hand rock to the left. Destroy the purple crystal and quickly dash across to the next **Heart Piece**.

Heart Piece 12/32

Mini rock puzzle, inside a cave.

(Tal Tal Mountain Range)

Collected?

Now go back down the steps, dash across and up the next steps, and go through the opening that's found in front of the two black crystals. Outside you'll find a chest that holds a **Purple Rupee**. Dash through the black crystals, then head outside again.

Walk right, then step inside the black entrance located just past the waving man. Dash up to the steps, climb them, watch out for the trapped chest, dash down, and speak to **Papahl** outside. Give him your **Pineapple** and he'll give you a **Hibiscus flower** in exchange.

Drop back down, go back into the stream, and dash right. Now drop down to the entrance of the fourth dungeon.

Fourth Dungeon: Angler's Tunnel

From the entrance, go up, then up the steps in front of you, dash right, go down the steps, and open the chest for this dungeon's **Stone Beak**.

Go back up the steps, then at the previous screen go up. Head right, then open up the chest here for this dungeon's **Map**. Go down the nearby steps and perform a dash jump across the gap.

Note

Dark blue patches of water are currently dangerous for you. Falling in now will cost you health. However, it is safe to walk around in the light blue patches (although your walking speed is reduced).

In this room, watch out for the **Water Tektites**, flying **Peahats**, and the **Bubbles**. Look for the cracked wooden block near the chest and throw a bomb at it. Run over to it, push the remaining block out of the way, and open the chest for a **Small Key**.

Go North and in the next screen, *stand still at the entrance* and throw a bomb at the cracked block in the middle. Open the chest to reveal a **Small Key**.

Make your way back to where you found the Map earlier, head towards the first room after the dungeon's entrance, and clear the enemies in the water. This opens up the doorway to the far right.

Clear every enemy you can in here to open up the bottom door. Open the chest here for the **Compass**. Go down into the open door and smash every purple crystal on the way to the chest. Open it for another **Small Key**. Clear the room of enemies to open the exit.

Use your key on the locked door to your right and again on the door in this room. In the next room, dash jump across the gap and open up the metal block here with your remaining small key.

Be careful of the **Shrouded Stalfo**s here as it can get annoying. Push the block in front of you up and clear out the remaining enemies (including the **Star**).

Go left, clear the enemies here and you'll see the Small Key fall straight down the hole and into some water! Oh no!

Go South and then head down to the bottom of this room ASAP. Turn left, follow the shallow path to the next screen on the left, head up, open the booby-trapped chest, then go up into the next room.

From here, go right, and open the chest in the next room to pocket a **Small Key**. Go left again, then down two screens, then right, then up (past the broken Owl statue), go up into the next room and open up the locked door.

Mini-Boss: Hydrosoar

The trick to this enemy is to let it charge at you and then jump over the top of it. Immediately turn around when you land and get a sword attack in. Repeat this six times (with the Red Mail on), or 12 times (with the Green or Blue Mail on).

In the next room, you must, very quickly, dodge the Spark and go into the left-hand door. Before the blocks close in and you then need to pull the long handle all the way back to reset the timer.

In this room, dispose of the **Gels** to stop the eyes firing fireballs at you, then open the chest to claim your next power-up: **The Flippers**!

Flippers

The flippers allow you to safely swim across the deep blue patches of water and also dive underwater. Keep this in mind, as diving will be required to find Hearts, other items, and even fight this dungeon's boss!

Go straight down into the next room to encounter a new enemy type, the **Helmasaur**. These creatures are only vulnerable to your sword from the back (as their front is protected).

Clear the room of enemies and then follow the ball of light for the correct order in which to stand on the grey tiles. This then opens up the top door again.

Note

The order in which these tiles flash changes for every playthrough. Therefore, it's *critical* that you pay very close attention! You must repeat the same order in an upcoming room with similar tiles!

For now, go South and then run to the bottom of the room. Jump into the deep water in the bottom right-hand corner and swim right. Jump out, keep heading right, push the left block to go down, dash jump across the gap, swim to the chest on the left and open it for a **Purple Rupee**. Swim back up, dash jump back across the same gap and then proceed down the steps.

Jump across the moving platform and swim down for the **Small Key** that's resting at the bottom of the water. Make your way back up the ladder to the upper floor again.

Make your way to the left, then in the next room go down, go left, jump into the deep water, swim to the chest here, and open it for another **Purple Rupee**.

Swim down, go left, keep heading left, then up (past the two Shrouded Galfos'), and into the room with the unlit floor tiles. Clear the room of Water Tektites and then *step on the tiles in the order that they flashed (see the note on the last page)*. A set of stairs will now appear, proceed on down them.

In the underground section, dash under the Thwomps, and then quickly climb the ladder so you can jump off of it and onto the top of the Thwomp.

If you make a mistake, don't worry, get close to the Thwomp to make it drop down again, giving you as many attempts as your health bar allows. Jump across to the other side, go up the ladder, then head down, open the chest, and pocket the **Nightmare Key**.

Go up, and for a shortcut, drop down in between the stone pillars to the wet floor below. Swim right, then swim up to and stand on the beige button by the locked door. Go up, open up the locked block, and head down the steps.

As you swim, attack each of the enemies with your sword. Climb up, push the block in, clear the room of Gels and then open up the boss door. Go down the steps, drop into the water, and swim down for this dungeon's boss fight!

Nightmare Boss Fight

Angler Fish

The best strategy here is to use charged spinning sword attacks as you can still swim around as the fish moves from right-to-left and left-to-right. Use the spinning attacks on its glowing orb above its head.

Watch out for the rocks that fall when it hits the wall at either side and also for the mini-fish that appear halfway through the battle (they only need 1-2 hits each). Keep up with the constant charged spinning attacks on its orb and this fight will be over in a couple of minutes.

Collect the **Heart Container** from the water, head up, and then pick up the **Surf Harp** in the next room.

Chapter 8

The Journey to the fifth dungeon

Item Collect-a-thon

Get ready to start collecting a lot of items before we get anywhere near the next dungeon! From the outside of the dungeon, go left and swim into the nearby door. Speak with **Mambo the fish** and you'll learn **Mambo's Mambo**. Exit the cave and start swimming right. You'll eventually see a door in the wall on your left. Enter it and dive down into the water to collect the next **Heart Piece**.

Heart Piece 13/32
Underwater, cave right of Angler's Tunnel.

(Tal Tal Heights)

Collected?

Exit the cave, swim down, then climb the steps to get back onto dry land. Stick to the lower-path and when you see the ladder leading down into the water, head down, and you'll now be at **Kanalet Castle**.

Stay in the water and start swimming left. At the junction swim up towards the small waterfall. Dive down to pick up the next **Secret Seashell**.

Secret Seashell 18/50
Under waterfall, North of Kanalet Castle.

(Kanalet Castle)

Collected?

Now swim down the left-side of the castle and then turn right at the bottom. When you get close to the castle's entrance, dive under the water to pick up the next **Heart Piece**.

Heart Piece 14/32

Underwater, left of the castle's main gate.

(Kanalet Castle)

Collected?

For now, ignore the pink ghost that's following you around and swim back up to the steps at the back of the castle. Dash down over the wooden bridge, go left, and then go inside the **Seashell Mansion**.

Come here after collecting a certain number of seashells for a reward (with 40 being the total amount you need to find for the "ultimate sword"). However, there's an additional reward given for finding all **50** Secret Seashells!

If you've been following our guide up to now, then the first prize you'll receive is a **Heart Piece**.

Heart Piece 15/32

Reward for finding five Secret Seashells.

(Seashell Mansion)

Collected?

If you've found over 10 Secret Seashells then you'll be rewarded with the **Seashell Sensor**. While it's designed to help you find the hidden seashells more easily, that's what our guide does (and is much more accurate - even if we *do* say so ourselves).

Leave the Seashell Mansion, go down the hill, take a right, then walk down the short steps and into the river. Swim South, swim around the corner, and the head up the steps in front of the row of six trees. Now head left into the maze of circular rocks, go down, and then left and into the cave entrance.

Run to the far left-hand wall and drop a bomb by the cracked wall. Be careful in the next room as there's a drop right by the entrance. Jump across the gap and walk up the steps.

61

Push the rock into the pit, jump across, walk around and then push the third rock from the bottom right one, then the rock above you up once space, allowing you to proceed. Now head outside again.

Go up to the Owl statue, clear the area of enemies, and then dig a hole to the left of the statue. The next **Secret Seashell** will pop up for you to collect.

Secret Seashell 19/50

Under a bush, left of the Owl statue.

(Ukuku Prairie)

Collected?

Go back inside the cave, go up the steps in front of you and drop down to the steps heading down. This time, after jumping across, go down immediately and you'll reappear outside at **Martha's Bay**.

Dash straight down and then turn left when you see the single pothole. Pick up the rock to reveal a small warp point. Go right, then down towards the steps that are opposite the phone hut. Swim around to the island, chop the bush, and pick up the next **Secret Seashell**.

Secret Seashell 20/50

Under a bush, on the tiny island.

(Martha's Bay)

Collected?

Go back onto dry land, turn right, and look for the nearby bush in the corner of some grass. Cut it to reveal another **Secret Seashell**!

Secret Seashell 21/50

Under a bush, right of the phone hut.

(Martha's Bay)

Collected?

Go down and you'll see a patch of potholes and some bushes. The best thing to do here is to do a dash jump across and then start attacking the bushes as you're jumping. If timed right, Link will cut a bush (but will likely fall down the hole). No matter, just dash across the same spot again and then head down the steps.

Swim around the corner but keep your eyes peeled for the familiar sight of a **Heart Piece** that's laying underwater. Make sure you dive down to pick it up!

Heart Piece 16/32

Underwater in a narrow cave tunnel.

(Martha's Bay)

Collected?

Go up the steps, dash across the grass, and then head down the next set of steps. Use your **Magic Powder** on the fire-pit here to awaken **Li'l Devil**. He'll punish you by allowing you to **carry more bombs**. How thoughtful of him!

Bomb Capacity Upgrade

Make sure that you don't miss out on securing this increase in the number of bombs you can carry. They'll definitely come in handy for later puzzles and bosses!

Retrace your steps, jump back across the potholes, walk past the Phone Hut, but go South at the single pothole. Dash jump across the three potholes and walk inside the hut with the purple roof.

Let the Ghost wander around, leave when asked, but then go back inside. Smash the pots to the right to reveal the next **Secret Seashell**.

Secret Seashell 22/50

Inside a pot, in the lost ghost's hut.

(Koholint Prairie)

Collected?

Step outside, bust out your Ocarina and play the Fish's warp tune. Now warp to **Manbo's Pond** (the closest warp point to the cemetery).

When you arrive, go up, pick up the rock to your left, then go towards the potholes, but then go down. Dash straight down, throw away the rock that's blocking the steps, and make your way to the patch of grass in front of you. Dig a hole in the middle for the next **Secret Seashell**.

Secret Seashell 23/50

Under the grass patch, ghosts gravestone.

(Koholint Prairie)

Collected?

Now to the sole gravestone that's surrounded by purple flowers. As a thank you for your troubles, the Ghost will give you an empty **Fairy Bottle**! Sweet!

Next Major Item: Bow and Arrow Set

However, the item collect-a-thon continues! Once Owl has finished chatting, pull out your Ocarina and warp to the **Animal Village**. Go to the top of the village and head into the hut that's the second from the top-right.

In here, speak with **Christine** at the desk. She'll trade your **Hibiscus** for a **Goat's Letter**.

Step back outside and dash left to **Martha's Bay**. Now dash North and go down the steps that are beside the stream.

Dash through the black crystals and dive into the pool of water below to find the next **Heart Piece**.

64

Heart Piece 17/32

Underwater in a different cave tunnel.

(Martha's Bay)

Collected? ☐

Go back up the steps, pull out your Ocarina once more, and warp to **Manbo's Pond**. Exit the warp tile, throw the nearby rock away, and head into the **Mysterious Forest**.

Stick to the top left-hand path and head past the open chest. Now when you reach the far left there'll be a junction above and below you. Ignore both and dig a hole at the base of the tree in front of you to reveal the next **Secret Seashell**.

Secret Seashell 24/50

Dig up the ground, top left-hand tree.

(Mysterious Forest)

Collected? ☐

Go up and into the next hut you see for Mr. Write's home. Hand him the **Goat's Letter** and he'll give you a **Broom** (after you learn a life lesson in not taking everyone at face-value).

Exit his home, go North towards the caves, but take a right towards the large wall. There's a lonely bush here that you can cut and then dig up to reveal a **Secret Seashell**.

65

Secret Seashell 25/50

Cut down the lonely bush, then dig.

(Goponga Swamp)

Collected?

Go back into the **Mysterious Forest** again and head right until you see the three rocks surrounding the tree trunk. Go down, take care of the Moblin, and then dig a hole in the middle of the patch of blue flowers. A **Secret Seashell** will reveal itself.

Secret Seashell 26/50

Dig up the middle of the blue flowers.

(Mysterious Forest)

Collected?

Go South to **Mabe Village**, speak to **Grandma Yahoo** who's standing outside her house. She'll take your **Broom** off your hands and give you a **Fishing Hook**.

Make sure you've got more than **980 rupees** on you before you go any further as you now need to buy the **Bow and Arrow Set** from the town's shopkeeper. Feel free to grind for rupees in the nearby grass and bushes if you're a little short (which you shouldn't be if you've been closely following this guide).

To the Fifth Dungeon

Leave the shop and go right to **Ukuku Prairie**, then step on the nearby Warp Tile, and warp to **Animal Village**.

Go back into **Christine's hut** and she'll thank you for giving Mr. Write the letter with a **Secret Seashell**.

Secret Seashell 27/50

Thank-you gift from Christine.

(Animal Farm)

Collected?

Leave her hut, dash left to **Ukuku Prairie**, and head into the large pool of water on the left by the trees (using the small set of steps beside the trees). Swim down and head under the wooden bridge. Jump onto the boat and trade your **Fishing Hook** for a **Necklace**.

Swim back out, go up, then swim left, and around the giant fish head. At the bottom, go down (you should see a **Mermaid statue** on your right as you do), and then you'll reach a dead-end of rocks. Dive down to pick up a **Heart Piece**.

Heart Piece 18/32

Underwater, South of the Mermaid statue.

(Martha's Bay)

Collected?

Now swim North and just up past the giant Zora statue and you'll see a **Mermaid**. Speak to her and she'll trade your **Necklace** for a **Scale**.

Now swim down to the giant **Zora statue** where you see rocks lined up like an entrance. When you reach the edge of the circle of rocks, **dive down** to enter a 2D swimming area. Swim across, then up, and enter the fifth dungeon.

Fifth Dungeon: Catfish's Maw

Upon entering the dungeon, go left into the first room. Run past the enemies into the second room, then clear the room of enemies here to open up the left-hand door that you should go through.

Open the chest to your right for the dungeon's **Compass**. Now proceed down the steps and when you stand on the chained 2D rock, wait a second for the other rock to rise up a bit. Now quickly jump across to the platform at the other side.

The next chained rock activates the middle-left rock. So, you need to raise that rock halfway, then jump onto the second rock until the rock closest to the ladder is high enough. Now quickly jump across all remaining rocks to reach the ladder.

In the next room, clear it of Stalfos' and purple crystals. Push the top two wooden blocks to the middle of the room to reveal a **Small Key**. Collect it, then head back down the steps you just came up from.

Run back through the 2D room, then in the next room, get rid of every enemy to make the door open. In the next room, open up the locked door with your small key.

In this room, immediately walk left, then clear the room of enemies to make the left-hand door open up. Proceed on through.

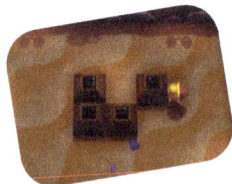

Use a clay pot on an enemy in here to get rid of it in one hit. Get rid of both enemies and a chest appears. Open it for the **Stone Beak**. Be sure you **grab the 10 bombs** floating here (you'll need them in a moment for an upcoming mini-boss battle).

Proceed two rooms to the right, then head up. Clear the room of enemies, switch to bombs, head up and into your first mini-boss battle for this dungeon...

Mini-Boss: Master Stalfos (Part 1)

68

This enemy isn't too hard to beat. Hit it with your sword once and, when it's laying on the ground, quickly drop a bomb. Dodge its leaping attacks, hit it, bomb it, and repeat until the fight's over.

Open the chest in the next room for an interesting… surprise. Now go up, push the block up, head left then immediately back into the previous room (this was to reset the position of the wooden blocks). Push the wooden block forwards, head up (to reset the blocks again), go back down, step on the big button to open the door, push the wooden block down, and then enter the right-hand door.

Mini-Boss: Master Stalfos (Part 2)

The tactics are almost identical as the last time. The only real difference is that you want to lure it into jumping at you. You get a second to attack it when it lands (which you don't get when it's walking around the room). It's a quick fight, so don't worry, you've got this.

Leave the room, go up, then go through the passage in the top-left. Lift the pot up that's directly in front of you and push the wooden block forward. Get rid of the Gels on both sides of this room to open up the door.

Mini-Boss: Master Stalfos (Part 3)

Use the exact same tactics as in the last fight. It really is that simple.

Exit the room using the left-hand door, clear the room of jumping Stalfos' and open the chest for the **Map**. Bust out your Ocarina and play the fish's warping tune and warp back to the entrance to save time.

Keep walking left, clearing the rooms, head down the steps to the 2D section again, pass through it once more, head up, and then proceed into the far-left room.

Mini-Boss: Master Stalfos (Part 4)

Once again, the method stays the same: Attack it after it jumps and bomb it (a total of three times). Do note though, that its jumping speed has increased, so you've got less time than before to react.

You'll be rewarded with your next major upgrade for your troubles: **The Hookshot**! Be sure to equip it (along with the **Roc Feather**).

69

Make your way back to the room with the four eye statues and the wooden blocks in it (near the two rooms away from the entrance). Go up and to the right this time and use your new-found hookshot to pull you across the gap to the chest. Open it for a cool Silver Rupee worth **100 rupees**. Nice! Hookshot back and go up.

Keep walking up, then turn right in the next room, then up, then left at the wooden blocks junction, then up where there's a room with deep water in the middle. Dive down to be taken to a 2D underwater section.

Swim across, then up, use your hookshot on the handle opposite you to create a long bridge. Open the chest to receive the **Nightmare Key**. Make your way back through the 2D section, and then head down when you resurface.

Go right, push the wooden block left, proceed upwards, and in the next room, walk around the two wooden blocks to your left and then use your hookshot to pull you to the wooden block in the bottom right-hand corner.

Use the hookshot to pull you to the chest here and open it for a Purple Rupee. Immediately go right, hookshot across, open the chest and take the **Small Key**.

Go back, then up and use the hookshot to pull across another makeshift bridge. Open this chest for another Purple Rupee. Equip your Ocarina and use it to warp back to the dungeon's entrance.

Go left twice, up, then left, then up. In this new room, go left, pull yourself across the gaps in the room, hookshot across to the chest and take the **Small Key** out of it. Leave through the bottom-right corner exit, hookshot back across this room, pull the bridge across, and proceed up into the next room.

Use the key on the locked metal block, switch to your bow and arrow (why else did you see loads of arrow refills floating around?) and you'll enter the next mini-boss room.

Mini-Boss: Gohma

The trick here is to dodge the lower Gohma when the upper Gohma stops to fire at you. You need to wait for both Gohma's to start shuddering as this is your queue that the the lower one is also getting ready to use a fireball on you.

Stand right in front of it, hold up your shield, block the fireball, and then immediately after, hit it with an arrow.

You can tell when a Gohma is going to use the dash attack instead as the eyelid will be *looking down*. If you see the eyelid stay up and start twitching, that's the time to stand in front of it, block, and then fire.

Be sure to time your shots as you only have 30 arrows. That may seem like a lot but, if you begin to panic, you can *easily* waste more than you realize. So, take your time, there's no rush.

Once they've both been defeated, equip your hookshot again, go right, down the steps then, in the 2D section, use your hookshot on the wooden panel above the ladder to pull you up to the ladder.

Use your final small key in the locked metal block, pull yourself across the gap and then get ready to take on the dungeon's boss!

Nightmare Boss Fight (Slime Eel)

Once the fight starts, begin walking around the room in an anti-clockwise direction (the same direction the spiked tail is spinning in).

When you see the boss is directly in front of you, quickly use your hookshot in its mouth to pull it towards you.

Now, very quickly, run down to the lit-up body part and hit it with your sword. If you're quick, you can get in five to six hits in each time.

After the first time, the tail will start spinning clockwise, so move round in this direction. After no more than eight hits with the Red Mail on (a few more if you have the Green or Blue Mail on), this dungeon's boss will be defeated!

Collect the **Heart Container**, go up into the next room, and pick up the **Wind Marimba** instrument.

71

Chapter 9

The Journey to the sixth dungeon

Completing the Trade Sub-Quest

Swim back under the dungeon's entrance, then go right, head up the small steps near the vertical row of trees, dash up, then run around the other side, and dash down towards the small wooden bridge that you had swam under.

Run up to the Owl statue and dig a hole to the left of it for a **Secret Seashell**.

> **Secret Seashell 28/50**
> Dig the ground, left of the Owl statue.
>
> (Martha's Bay)
>
> **Collected?**

Now go down, and opposite the wooden bridge you were just on there are some steps. Near the steps there's a wooden post. Use your hookshot to pull you across to the other side. Head up and place the **Scale** on the **Mermaid Statue**.

This causes some steps to appear, so head down them. Walk up and claim your prize for completing the trading sub-quest: A **Magnifying Lens**!

To the Ancient Ruins

Head back out, pull yourself back across the gap, and then head to the top right-hand house in **Animal Village**. Speak to the Zora (that you can now only see because you have the Magnifying Lens) and he'll bribe you with a **Secret Seashell** in order to stay quiet about him being there.

Secret Seashell 29/50

Speak to the invisible Zora, top-right home.

(Animal Village)

Collected?

Head out of Animal Village, but immediately go South, then East, and when you reach the wooden signpost, dash North. Drop a bomb at the cracked wall, push the right-hand block down, use your hookshot on the enemy to stun it, then jump across and knock it off of the ledge.

Now, use a bomb on the cracked wall here, clear the path of enemies, and throw a bomb over the smaller stones to it lands in front of the cracked rock on the other side. Now go back through the hole in the wall, head left, and when you reach the room with the **Heart Piece** in it, you can now hookshot across to collect it.

Heart Piece 19/32

Inside a cave, bomb the N/E corner.

(Animal Village)

Collected?

Exit the cave, take out your Ocarina and warp to **Martha's Bay**. Go down and dash jump across the three potholes. Go up and left and lift up the rocks to be back at **Toronbo Shores**.

Head left a screen, then go down when the beach opens up. Equip your bombs and blow a hole in the cracked part of the wall.

Note

You need to trade an item that's equipped to either the X or Y button. We recommend that you trade your Shovel. Just make sure you have 300 Rupees spare *before* you do so (as you can leave his shop and buy it right back off of him)!

73

Speak to **Goriya** and give him your **Shovel** (don't worry, you can come back and swap your items back again. Or, you can buy it back from him for 300 rupees). In return, you'll be given the **Boomerang**! The Boomerang is very useful for stunning enemies Now use your Ocarina to warp to the **Seashell Mansion**.

Boomerang

The Boomerang is a very versatile item. Not only can it be used to stun enemies (which can often be finished off with a second hit), but it can also be used to collect multiple smaller items that are far away from you (such as rupees and heart refills)! Sweet!

Run down the hill, go left, then down (near the hollow rocks), now go right towards the wooden sign, equip your Feather and your Hookshot, and pull yourself across the water using the tree stumps.

Go North, then East and the Owl will stop you to chat. Continue right, then lift up the rocks in your way, equip your new Boomerang, and go down at the junction.

Ancient Ruins

Note

Touching some of the statues in this area brings them to life. This is often required as some of them are intentionally blocking off your path. Hit them *twice* with your Boomerang to dispose of them quickly!

Keep walking down to the bottom, walk into the statue in front of you and dispose of it when it comes to life. Go left, then up and walk into the top-left corner statue. Deal with it, continue left, then go up.

Go up and take the right-hand path. Clear the statue out of your way, then push into the bottom-right statue to reveal a set of steps going down. Inside the cave is the next **Secret Seashell**!

Secret Seashell 30/50

Inside a secret cave, under a statue.

(Ancient Ruins)

Collected?

Go back, keep going left (stay close to the wall above you), dispatch the statue in your way, and work your way around this one-way path to reach the large stone building. Once inside, walk down the steps to encounter a rather large enemy...

Mini-Boss: Amos Knight

This isn't a difficult fight. Use charged sword attacks and then jump just before the knight lands back on the ground. Once it the knight lands it'll stop for a second, so use this time to get reasonably close and do a spin attack with your sword. Keep this pattern up of jumping when it lands and hitting it afterwards to make short work of it. You'll be rewarded with the **Face Key** for your trouble.

Head up into the next room, use your **Magic Powder** on the unlit lanterns and check out the painting for a real (cliched) plot twist.

Head back outside, chat with the Owl about this revelation, then make your way back through the entirety of the **Ancient Ruins**. Once you reach the maze of hollow rocks, lock for the rocks that you can lift in the middle.

Make your way up through the maze and when you see the lone rock in the top right-hand corner, lift it up, and claim the Secret Seashell underneath.

Secret Seashell 31/50

Under a rock, North of the Ancient Ruins.

(Martha's Bay)

Collected? ☐

Continue going left through the maze and when you reach the two sets of steps by the water, go up towards the dead-end. Blow a hole up in the wall with a bomb and step inside to reveal a new **Fairy Queen** location.

Leave, go down the steps in front of you into the water. Swim to the rectangular island with the two statues on it, push the left-hand statue and get rid of it before going down the steps.

Head past the cave pool, hookshot across the gap, head up to the next floor, and you'll reappear outside the entrance to the next dungeon. The keyhole is up to your left, so use your key. Now go inside the sixth dungeon and get that instrument!

Warning! On the chance that you haven't been following this guide closely, then you may not know that you're really going to want either the **Boomerang** (see the part about **Goriya** - earlier in this very chapter), or the **Bow and Arrow** (Mabe Village shop for 950 rupees) before you enter this dungeon (seriously - we're *not* joking).

Sixth Dungeon: Face Shrine

Head left from the entrance and stand at the top-right corner of the top-right torch to dodge the attacks from the **Wizzrobes**.

> **! Top Tip!**
> You can get rid of the Wizzrobes by hitting each one twice with your boomerang! They're as easy at that!

Go left and up, left, then use a charged sword attack on the Shy Guy here.

Stand on the top-right orange square and then fire your Boomerang diagonally down at the blue crystal to turn it orange and raise the tile you're standing on. Now head up.

Equip your bombs and use one on the cracked wall to your right. Head through, clear the room of all **Gels**, then head down the steps that appear.

Watch out for those glowing green **Giant Bubbles** that are here. So, take your time to wait for them to pass over you. Jump across the ladders to the other side and go up.

In this room, use your Boomerang on the Wizzrobes to stun them long enough for you to hit them with your sword. Clear both of them then head up into the next room.

Climb the steps, open the chest, and then claim your next major item upgrade, the **Powerful Bracelet**.

> **★ Power Bracelet**
> This bracelet allows you to lift those giant elephant statues you see littered throughout this dungeon! There's no need to manually equip the Power Bracelet, it's active all the time.

So, do just that to the elephant statues in front of you and go up. Spin attack the Shy Guy here, turn the crystal blue, and stand on the top-left orange tile before throwing a Boomerang diagonally at the crystal to turn it orange again.

Break the top-left pot in this room, to reveal a hidden floor switch. Step on it to open the nearby door. Use the Boomerang in the next room to clear it of all three Wizzrobes. A chest appears containing the dungeon's **Map**.

Continue up into the next room, go up, follow the path right, and claim the **Stone Beak** from the chest. Go back, lift a pot, and use it to smash the locked door open.

Go up, then right, claim the **Compass** from the chest, hit the crystal, go round to the right, jump into the flying bombs to stock up, go down, then right, then up, and clear the room using your Boomerang and sword to cause a **Small Key** to drop down.

Go back round to the room with the two large elephants and the Spark. Use the elephant statue to break open the door. Nice!

The chest in the next room has a **Silver Rupee** in it worth **100 rupees**. Sweet! Go up the steps and open the chest outside for a **Secret Seashell**.

Secret Seashell 32/50

Outside, on an island (climb the NW stairs).

(Face Shrine Dungeon)

Collected?

Mini-puzzle time. Go back down and in this room. Now, think of the floor tiles here as a chess board. The Knights move in accordance with how they can be moved in a game of chess. So, stand pick up the White Knight and stand on the white square that's to the right of the locked door (see the screenshot below for guidance). Throw it at the right-hand green square.

Pick up the Black Knight, stand on the black square on the right-side of the locked door (again, see the screenshot if you're unsure of where) and throw it at the left-hand green square.

Keep going down until you reach the room with the crystal in it. Stand on the lower-right orange square, and use your boomerang to hit the crystal, turning it orange.

Now it's time for a tricky move. Throw it back at the crystal and, *while the Boomerang is still in flight*, run up and off the **orange** tile so you're heading towards the right-hand door. This causes the **blue** tiles to raise after you pass them. Sneaky huh!?

Continue down, turn the crystal **orange**, and use the elephant statue to break open the locked door. Open the chest in the next room for a **Silver Rupee**. Go down and claim the **Purple Rupee** from the next chest.

Go down, then right (so you're back to the dungeon's entrance) and use your feather to jump across the moving floor (dodging the Blade Traps in the process).

Ah, we remember this next room well from the Gameboy original. Simply pick a corner of the room, hold up your shield, and let the tiles smash themselves on your shield. Job done!

Go up, smash open the pot door on the right, clear the room, head down, go up the steps, drop down onto the raised orange tile, then – very carefully – jump across the gap to the top of the next orange tile. Go up, jump over the Blade Trap, head up the path, and open the chest for a handy **Secret Medicine**.

Note

The Secret Medicine item works by automatically refilling all of your energy should you lose all of your health (effectively giving you a "1-Up." Although, you can only carry one at a time (any more are put back into their chest).

Drop down, go up, then proceed around the next room (there's only one path), go up, and take the **Small Key** from the chest.

Go back around to the nearby room with the locked door, open it, clear out the next room, and blow a hole in the wall opposite.

Mini-Boss: Rover

Alright, it's time to play some dodgeball with this enemy! Run to the opposite side of the screen from it, lower your shield, and it will through its ball at you.

79

Quickly lift up your shield, causing it to drop down. Now very quickly pick up the ball and throw it back at Rover.

Repeat this step (baiting it to throw the ball, raise your shield, and throwing it back), two more times to end the fight.

> **Top Tip!**
> If you're quick enough, you can get to the ball first after hitting the mini-boss. Effectively preventing it from ever getting the ball again, substantially speeding up the fight!

In the next room, lift up the left-hand statue and head down the steps. Use your Boomerang to get rid of the Sparks, jump across, and climb up the last ladder.

Immediately head down to the bottom right-hand corner and raise your shield, waiting here for every moving tile to dash at you and break. Now, very carefully, jump across the gaps to reach the **Small Key** that dropped down, and use it to open the metal block in this room.

Go up, smash the door here with the statue, head through, clear the pots, and use the location of where the pots where to throw the Black and White Knights onto the green tiles, opening the locked door.

Dash straight under the Thwomps, then dash off of the raised platform under the next set of Thwomps. Proceed up the ladder.

Use arrows on the **Pols Voices** in this room to make light work of them, go up, use your Boomerang on the Sparks, continue up, and then throw a Boomerang at the crystal to turn it blue. Grab the *Gold Rupee* from the chest for a cool **300 rupees**!

Once again, throw the two Knights in their L-Shaped path so they land on the *green* tiles, then hit the crystal with your Boomerang once more to turn it *orange*. Now keep going South until you encounter a mini-boss you've already met elsewhere...

Mini-Boss: Dodongo Snakes

The same strategy from before applies here. It's tougher due to the two rectangular gaps in the middle, but you still need to throw a bomb into their oncoming path (otherwise, they won't swallow it). Anticipate their movement, throw the bomb at their mouth *just* as it opens, and after three bombs each, they'll both be goners.

Exit through the left-hand door, equip your hookshot, pull yourself across the gap, and open up the locked block. Head up and then throw a pot at the chest to open it. The **Nightmare Key** pops out and into your hands.

Dash down, then drop down into the water below. Leave this room, go left, then up, keep going up (past the warp portal), and then in the next room, go down the steps.

Jump across the 2D platforms, climb the ladder up, head down through the Southern door, run around the edges of the room and let the Vacuum Mouth suck up all the Gels (opening the door for you).

Use two Boomerang shots on the Wizzrobe, and push the right-hand wooden block out of the way, then jump across, quickly push the other right-hand wooden block out of the way, and then head up (dodging any laser beams shot at you from the rotating eye).

In the next room, switch to your Bombs, then open up the door to the boss' room.

Nightmare Boss Fight

The boss' weak spot is its mouth. You need to drop, or throw, your bombs so they land by its mouth. You can quickly plant a bomb on its mouth as soon as it's finished talking. But make sure you get your shield up and face the top-right corner of the room, as this stops the tiles from damaging you (they'll just bounce off of your shield like before).

Once every tile has attacked you, stand where you are and throw your bombs over at its mouth. After your second hit, the boss will move around the room and random tiles will start disappearing. You need to juggle throwing bombs in the boss' direction, while also keeping Link out of the holes.

After you hit it with six bombs, the fight finishes. Collect the **Heart Container** and then head up and collect the **Coral Triangle**. Congratulations on beating the sixth dungeon!

There's still *loads* of collectables left to grab as we get ready to tackle the last two major dungeons. We hope you're ready…

Chapter 10

The Journey to the seventh dungeon

Riding the Rapid Rafts

Drop down into the water on the right, swim across to the steps, go up and then immediately go down the steps opposite and sim across to the right. Walk up the steps that are close to the waterfall and go inside the cave.

Swim across the water, hookshot across to the stone and then hookshot again across to the **Heart Piece**.

Heart Piece 20/32

Inside a cave, N/E of the sixth dungeon.

(Rapids Ride Cave)

Collected?

Now climb up the steps and you'll reemerge in **Tal Tal Heights**. Go down and enter the bamboo-covered **Raft Shop**.

Note

It's important to understand that the raft section is "on-rails." Once you get on the raft, you can't stop it. So, if you want to save rupees (and frustration), we recommend that you read ahead so you're prepared to make the right moves in time.

Rapids Raid

Make sure your **Roc Feather** is equipped for this as you'll be frequently jumping and your **hookshot**, as it required to pull you through the optimal route for collecting every key item (as it'll pull you against the strong current).

Begin by pulling yourself to each wooden pole with your hookshot. Make sure you don't go down the first mini-waterfall.

82

Instead, go down the second one and begin hooking on to the green vines on the left. You want to go down the left-hand path (by the wall).

Pull yourself into the vine that's located by the steps and head up for the next **Heart Piece**.

Heart Piece 21/32

Take the left path, found on a small island.

(Rapids Ride)

Collected?

Get back on your raft and control the raft so it reaches the platform with the Owl statue and the chest on it. Open the chest for a **Red Rupee**.

After getting back on the raft and going right, look for some hovering arrows. Pull yourself down towards the tree (using the green vines), then pull yourself to the green vines by the hovering **Red Rupee**.

Go up and step off onto the empty island surrounded by vines. Dig a hole in the top-right corner for a **Secret Seashell**.

Secret Seashell 33/50

Dig the ground on the empty island.

(River Rapids)

Collected?

Get back on your raft and head left. Go to the far left (by the wall) and there's a load of items hovering here for you to jump up and collect.

Stick to the bottom of the course and then use the hookshot to pull you to the green trees. This makes it easier to get the three hovering rupees in a row. You can also fire your hookshot diagonally to reach the four hovering items at the far-right side.

Once you drop down the waterfall, tell the Raft Shop Owner that you want to play the **Rapids Race** this time.

83

Rapids Race

Your Hookshot is essential if you want to make it around the course in under **40 seconds** (the time you need to reach, or beat, in order to earn a **Heart Piece**) or **35 seconds** (for a **Secret Seashell**).

Begin by pulling yourself to each of the wooden posts and then push yourself down the first waterfall. Pull yourself to the trees, and then at the junction, take the lower route.

Go straight down (nudging Link's raft to battle the current as required), then go left, and take the first path that opens up to the lower half of the rapids (look for the row of vines shaped like an "L").

Now use your hookshot to pull yourself to the right and up as fast as you can. If you finished the race in under 40 seconds, you obtain a **Heart Piece**. If you finished without getting stuck on the scenery and make it there in 35 seconds (or less), he'll reward you with a **Secret Seashell** for your valiant efforts.

Heart Piece 22/32
Finish the river race in under 40-seconds.

(Rapids Ride)

Collected?

Secret Seashell 34/50
Finish the river race in under 35-seconds.

(River Rapids)

Collected?

If you complete the River Rapids in under *30 seconds*, then you'll be rewarded with a Chamber Stone.

We'll be handing these to a character you may not have met yet. There's a total of fourteen of these to find. Don't worry, near the end of this guide we've included a chapter dedicated to the location of every **Chamber Stone** (Chapter 12).

Chamber Stone 01/14

Finish the river race in under 30-seconds.

(River Rapids)

Collected? ☐

The Final Ocarina Song

Once you've earned the Secret Seashell (or Chamber Stone), you can decline to play again and step off the raft onto dry land. Now warp to the **Secret Seashell Mansion** and it's time to cash in some of those well-earned seashells!

Step on the switch and you'll be rewarded with a **Chamber Stone**. Leave the hut, go down, then left, then up, then left (towards the telephone tree hut), then down, and dash left towards the large pool of water that surrounds the second dungeon's entrance.

Chamber Stone 02/14

Reward for collecting 30 Secret Seashells.

(Secret Seashell Mansion)

Collected? ☐

There's a lone bush on a rectangular island. Chop the bush and you'll reveal a **Secret Seashell**.

Secret Seashell 35/50

On the small island, N/E of Key Cavern.

(Ukuku Prairie)

Collected? ☐

Go back the way you came, but when you head up (just before the telephone hut), head up the nearby ladder and down the steps. Equip your shovel and dig to the South-West of the hollow rock that's near the step for a **Secret Seashell**.

Secret Seashell 36/50

Underneath the skull rock you blow up.

(Ukuku Prairie)

Collected?

Go back up the steps, down the ladder, past the telephone hut, and then go up near the bridge to **Kanalet Castle**. Instead of going on the bridge, look behind the trees on the left for a path with potholes. Use your hookshot to pull yourself across and then go down the steps. Open the chest for a **Secret Seashell**.

Secret Seashell 37/50

Left of the Kanalet Castle bridge

(Ukuku Prairie)

Collected?

Head outside and warp to the **Ukuku Prairie** warp tile. Equip your hookshot, go left (past the telephone hut), go down, then use your hookshot to cross the potholes to the other side. Now it's time to read some signs (in the correct order)!

Note

The solution to the upcoming puzzle changes from file to file. Meaning that we're unable to give you a set path. Therefore, you *must* follow the direction of the signs *exactly* as written. Also, make sure you also have 300 rupees available with you.

Some signs might *look* like they're the right one, but the next sign will - 100% of the time - be horizontally or vertically opposite the previous sign. You will have to navigate around obstacles to reach many of them but keep a mental image of where the last sign lined up. If you make a mistake, just return to the first signpost, and start again.

Once you've made it to the last signpost, you'll be pointed towards some stairs that have magically appeared in the ground. Go down, speak to the frog here and pay him **300 rupees** to learn a new song for your Ocarina: ***Frog's Song of Soul***.

Seashell and Heart Piece Bonanza

Once back outside, warp to **Animal Village**. Go to **Yarna Desert**, then proceed to the Owl statue in the North-Eastern corner. Dig a hole in the middle of the cacti directly opposite the Owl statue for a **Secret Seashell**.

Secret Seashell 38/50

Dig a hole opposite the Owl statue.

(Yarna Desert)

Collected?

Warp to **Ukuku Prairie**, go directly to **Mabe Village**, walk to the weather-vane, and push it up to reveal a secret set of stairs. Use your newly learned **Frog's Song of Soul** on the skull to bring the rooster back to life! Now go down to the **Trendy Game** hut.

You need to grab a couple of things while you're here. First, be sure to pick up the **Secret Seashell** (which only appears once you beat the sixth dungeon). Next, collect the **CiaoCiao Figure**, leave the Trendy Game hut, but *immediately* re-enter it again.

Your goal here is to pick up the **Chamber Stone**. Once collected, leave the hut and *immediately* re-enter it again. Your next goal is to pick up the **Heart Piece**. Collect it, leave the hut, then re-enter it again and you can now pick up *another* **Secret Seashell**! Phew! That's a *lot* of items!

Secret Seashell 39/50
Trendy game prize (after sixth Dungeon).

(Mabe Village)

Collected?

Chamber Stone 03/14
Trendy Game Prize.

(Mabe Village)

Collected?

Heart Piece 23/32
Trendy Game Prize.

(Mabe Village)

Collected?

Secret Seashell 40/50
Trendy game prize.

(Mabe Village)

Collected?

Leave the hut (for real this time) and then head North from CiaoCiao's hut to the **fisherman standing by the lake**. There's quite a few goodies to earn here for a spot of fishing.

> ## Top Tip!
>
> There's no need to rush things while you're luring the fish towards your bait. For bigger fish, pull it in for a few seconds, let go, and a second after it begins pulling away, reel it back in for a few more seconds. Rinse and repeat until caught.

After cashing your first fish, you'll earn some rupees and a **Heart Piece** for your troubles.

Heart Piece 24/32

Catch a small fish.

(Mabe Village)

Collected? ☐

Play again, but this time, throw the line as far left as you can. Now let the lure sink to the bottom of the lake and drag it right. About halfway across it should get caught on something. Start reeling in your line and you'll notice that you've caught an empty **Fairy Bottle**!

Play again and you'll now notice a *much* bigger fish has joined the mini-game. And it's *far* harder to catch as it's not as interested in a small lure as the smaller fish are. So, for now at least, aim to hook the slightly larger green fish. It'll put up more of a fight, so learn to pull it in a bit, pause for a second, and then reel it in some more, pause, then repeat this until you've caught it.

The fisherman is so impressed, he'll hook you up with a better, well, hook – a **Middleweight Lure**. This is what you need to catch that bigger fish. He'll also reward you with *another* **Heart Piece**!

Heart Piece 25/32

Catch a bigger fish.

(Mabe Village)

Collected?

Alright, for the bigger fish, the challenge isn't just with catching it. The better lure is also *far* more attractive to the smaller fish (increasing the odds of you catching one of the smaller fish by accident). So, you need to be very deliberate in getting the lure to sink to the bottom of the lake where the big fish is.

You also need to play the long game when reeling it in. As before, reel it in for a bit, give it a second or two to pull away and settle down, then reel it back in for a couple of seconds, let it pull away slightly, reel it back in some more, and repeat until you've caught it. Just be patient, it may take you a few tries to get.

When you finally catch Ol' Baron (that weighs more than 60lbs), you'll be rewarded with **120 Rupees** and **TWO Chamber Stones**! Wow!

Chamber Stone 04/14

Catch Ol' Baron (under 60lbs)

(Mabe Village)

Collected?

Chamber Stone 05/14

Catch Ol' Baron (*over* 60lbs)

(Mabe Village)

Collected?

Ask the fisherman to play again and your goal now is to catch the Blooper that's bobbing around the water. It'll put up a fight, but your reward is a **Heavyweight Lure** and a **Secret Seashell**.

Secret Seashell 41/50

Catch a Blooper Fish.

(Mabe Village)

Collected?

You'll want to keep playing, and catching fish, until you see a brown **Cheep-Cheep** fish appear (it's another Mario game enemy cameo appearance). The reward for catching the Cheep-Cheep is a S**ecret Seashell**.

Secret Seashell 42/50

Catch a Cheep-Cheep Fish.

(Mabe Village)

Collected?

With your sizeable haul of Hearts and Seashells now tucked away safely, it's time to move on. Make sure you've got at least **200 Rupees** in your wallet (if not, go back and catch more fish until you do), then head back to the **Town Tool Shop** and pick up the **Heart Piece** here and buy it for **200 rupees**.

Heart Piece 26/32

Costs 200 Rupees, Town Tool Shop.

(Mabe Village)

Collected?

If you've been following this guide closely, then you'll have found over **40** secret seashells. If you do indeed have 40 (or more), now's a great time to warp to the **Seashell Mansion**. Stand on the button this time and you'll be rewarded with a **Chamber Stone** for collecting **30** seashells! Nice!

Chamber Stone 06/14

Collect 30 Secret Seashells.

(Seashell Mansion)

Collected?

You'll also be rewarded with the **Koholint Island Sword**! *This sword is the most powerful sword in the game!* Making your life *much* easier for the final two dungeons.

Don't worry though, we'll still show you the location of the remaining 10 Secret Seashells (earning you the next reward in the process).

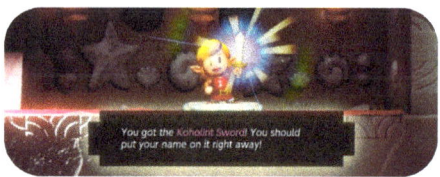

Top Tip!

Not only is the Koholint Sword more powerful than your regular sword, it also emits powerful projectile beams if you're at full health *and* it's strong enough to break those clay pots with a single swipe. Sweet!

Exit the shop, go up into the **Mysterious Forest**, and then head into the wooden tree stump that's surrounded by the three rocks.

Use your hookshot to reach the chest (that contains a **Purple Rupee**), and then push the rock down to access the **Heart Piece**. Use your feathered-friend to quickly fly back to the exit.

92

Heart Piece 27/32

Inside the blocked-off wooden tree stump.

(Mysterious Forest)

Collected?

To the Next Dungeon's Key

Exit the **Mysterious Forest** to the right, head North towards the swamp, go right, lift the rocks at the sign, keep going right (by the edge of the mountain wall), climb up the second wooden ladder (found just before an apple tree), chat to the Owl, then lift up the rocks, and head inside the cave in **Tal Tal Mountain Range**.

Go right, then down the steps, head up the next set of steps, fly across the gap to the chest for a **Purple Rupee**, fly back, dash through the black crystals, then head out of the cave.

Dash right, past the dungeon entrance, and swim towards the mini waterfall. Dive down here to find a **Secret Seashell**.

Secret Seashell 43/50

Under the waterfall, past Angler Dungeon.

(Tal Tal Mountain)

Collected?

Now climb up the nearby wooden ladder and head inside the nearby cave entrance. When you reach the rock pushing puzzle, save yourself the time and hassle by picking up the rooster and using it to fly you around the left-hand side of the wall, before flying right towards the opening at the top of the room. Easy!

Fly around the gap in the next room, drop down at the steps, then collect the **Bird Key**. Now fly back and exit the route through which you came.

To the Eagle's Tower Dungeon

Go right, over the bridge, down the wooden ladder, swim right, then enter the cave opening. Select your bombs, blow a hole in the cracked Northern wall, go up the next set of steps, push the left-hand rock out of the way, then the rock South of you, and exit the cave. Open the nearby chest to reveal a **Secret Seashell**.

Secret Seashell 44/50

In a chest, en-route to the Eagle Dungeon.

(Tal Tal Mountain)

Collected?

When you head inside again, you need to open up four enemy-filled chests before you open the last one on the far-right (which contains a **Silver Rupee** if you solve this mini-puzzle).

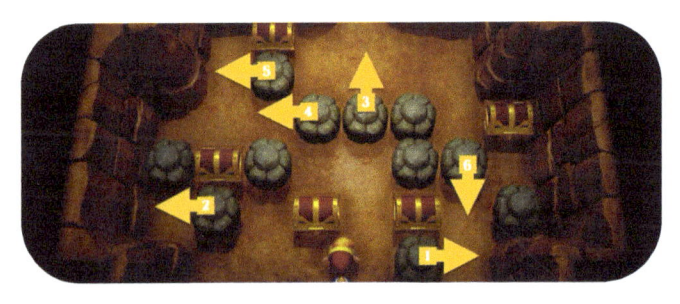

Proceed back down the steps and head right after passing back through the bombed wall. When outside, climb the ladder, then go inside the mountain caves again.

Dash right, head back outside, then go back inside via the next doorway. Go down the steps, jump across the gap, go up, right, then down, pull yourself across the gap with your hookshot, go down, and outside. Once outside, dig in between the middle of the four sets of pebbles to reveal a mini **Warp Portal**.

Now look out for the nearby broken piece of wall that you can blow up with a bomb. Inside you'll find a hidden **Fairy Fountain**. Very easy to warp to if you need a spare Fairy in a bottle (or two).

Work your way through the cave to the exit, lead left, lift up the rock that's in front of the keyhole and use your Bird Key to open up the entrance to the next dungeon – **Eagle's Tower**.

94

Seventh Dungeon: Eagle's Tower

Immediately upon entering, go right, jump across the enemies and spikes, go right once more, equip your boomerang, and then clear this room of enemies to earn a **Small Key**. Now open up the nearby door, then head up the steps to the next floor.

Go up (past the orange tiles), and then – very quickly – make it past the moving blocks on the left. If you're too slow, pull the handle on the far right to 'reset the timer' on the blocks. Deliberately fall down the pit in front of you and you'll reappear in a room on the floor below.

Dash across the orange tiles to the left, cross the next room, then go down when the orange tiles go up and down. Open the chest here for this dungeon's **Stone Beak**.

Go back up one screen, dash right across the orange tiles again, keep going right, and then use your boomerang on the blue crystal to lower the blue tiles.

Go left, then follow the blue tiles down, then right, go down, go back through the door you opened up earlier, and proceed back up to the next floor. Open up the chest here to reveal a new major item – the **Mirror Shield**!

Mirror Shield

This mirror shield allows you to reflect back those annoying beams that are fired by the rotating pillars. Stand to face the pillar and the reflected beam will bounce back, in turn, destroying the pillar! Nice!

Take a look at where the orange crystal is and drop down the gap beside it. You'll land on a narrow platform on the floor below. Go North and keep going until you reach a chest. Open it for a **Small Key**. Dash down two screens, then go back up the steps to the next floor.

Use your boomerang on the orange crystal, go up, pick up the black ball, drop it in front of the moving gray blocks, then pull the handle back all the way to reset the timer. Pick the black ball back up before you go left.

95

Carefully throw the black ball at the cracked pillar in the room to break it. Go up, throw the knights onto the squares, and open the chest that appears for the dungeon's **Map**.

It's now time for a cheeky trick. Go down into the room that had the pillar and stand in between the pit and the blue tile nearest the pit. Look towards the bottom right-hand corner of the room and jump across from one corner of the pit to the other side. If you fall into the pit (to the floor below), make your way back up here and try it again.

Once you make it, go down two screens, hit the crystal, go back up, pick up the black ball, go back down, and break the pillar in here with the ball.

Pick the ball back up, go up one screen, drop the ball down, push the wooden block on the left away, pick the ball back up, and take it left with you.

Throw it over the spikes, jump across, and take the ball with you up, then across and down, and throw it over the small wooden barrier.

Go back up, clear this room of the **Three-of-a-Kinds** and open the chest for this dungeon's **Compass**. Now go down through the bottom right-hand exit and fall down the pit at the bottom of this narrow corridor with the spikes and wooden blocks in it.

You'll land on top of the raised orange tiles. Go up (onto the blue tiles), dash left, go down, then up the steps to the next floor. Go left, enter the rotating doorway, clear the Bubble, then stand in a corner with your shield up, and let the tiles destroy themselves.

Go right, break the pillar with the ball, plant a bomb in the Southern wall (in between the two sets of lanterns), push the wooden block into the square gap, pick up the ball, and then throw it across the gap to the bottom right-hand exit. Jump across the gap, pick up the ball, and go right.

Drop the ball, move the block, now take the ball with you again and go down one screen. Go down once more and throw the ball over the small barrier (just past the crystal).

Go back up, push the block out of the way (again), go left, fall down the square hole in front of you, dash left, go down, then back up the stairs to the next floor.

Now go left, back up through the rotating door, and wait for the top-left tile to fly at you and then fall down the hole it creates. After landing on the narrow path, go up, and open the chest for a **Secret Seashell**!

Secret Seashell 45/50

In a chest, left side of Eagle Dungeon.

(Eagle's Tower)

Collected?

Run down two screens, then jump off to the right when you reach the room with the opened chest and the steps leading up. Go back up the steps to the next floor, equip your bow and arrows, and then head down to the next room.

Mini-Boss: Hinox

You can make very light work of this enemy by quickly firing off a barrage of arrows while it takes its time to turn around and face you. Pick up the **Small Key** that drops.

Take the right-hand path, clear the Three-of-a-Kind enemies out of the way (to make a chest appear in the room), go right, pick up the ball, throw the ball over the smaller barriers, across the pit, to the other side of the room.

Go left, up, up through the revolving door at the top, right, down through the hole you blasted in the wall earlier, blow up the wall at the end of this room, pull yourself across the gap (using the chest and your hookshot), collect the ball, go up, and knock down the fourth – and final – pillar.

After the brief cut-scene, go down, and fall into the pit. Now go right, right again, enter the door, go up the steps, go down, open up the locked metal block, head up the steps, drop down the other side, use your boomerang on the crystal (lowering the *orange* tiles), then head up the steps to the next floor.

Go up, right, stand by the door, and get ready for a, rather simple, mini-boss battle.

Mini-Boss: The Grim Creeper

Simply stand by the door you entered and slash away with your sword until all of the enemies are gone. That's it!

Proceed North into the next room, push the two wooden blocks towards the middle of the room to reveal a chest. Open it to obtain the **Nightmare Key**.

Now go down, left, dash through the **Goombas**, and use the key on the boss door. Go up the steps, pull yourself across to the wooden post on the right, go down one screen, then take the steps up on your right.

Equip your bow and arrows before climbing up the ladder to the boss fight.

Nightmare Boss Fight

This boss begins by flying overhead at high speed. If you aim upwards, you can often hit it with an arrow by firing just before it reaches half-way across the screen.

After a successful hit, the Eagle pauses for a brief second. Make the most of this by rapidly firing off another three to four arrows.

The Eagle will now come down and swipe at you with its talons. Make sure to block these and then, after two swipes, retaliate by hitting it with your sword.

When it starts flapping its wings at you, now's the time to start dashing towards the Eagle to prevent yourself from being blown off the top.

When the Eagle passes by at a much lower height, this is a great opportunity to fire off loads of arrows into it!

Block the next set of talon attacks and your retaliation with your sword should be enough to finish this fight once and for all.

Collect your **Heart Container**, climb back down the ladder, drop down the ledge to the door that's surrounded by the wooden blocks, and pick up the **Organ of Evening Calm**.

Chapter 11

The Journey to the eighth dungeon

To Turtle Rock

Upon exiting the dungeon, drop off the top of the nearby right-hand edge, go into the right-hand doorway, head around the cave, then you'll come out in **Tal Tal Mountain Range** again.

Head into the doorway just past the Owl statue, go through this tunnel, swim past the mini waterfall, climb up the nearby ladder, head left, walk up the steps (in front of the hut), then go right.

Jump across the gap in the wooden bridge and lift up all the rocks to reveal a **Secret Seashell**.

Secret Seashell 46/50

Under a rock, by the broken bridge.

(Tal Tal Mountain Range)

Collected?

Go back across the broken bridge, then stop at the start of the left-hand wooden bridge (close to the hut). Look down for a round hole. Throw a bomb down this hole and you'll blow up a **Secret Seashell**.

Secret Seashell 47/50

Blow it out of the round hole with a bomb.

(Tal Tal Mountain Range)

Collected?

Pull yourself across the massive gap to the other side of the bridge, hookshot across (pulling **Marin** with you this time), and let the short scene play out. Once you regain control of Link, hack at the nearby bush to reveal some steps going down.

Equip your bombs and plant a bomb in the Southern alcove (close to the steps). Go in, then right, and pick up the **Heart Piece** inside.

Heart Piece 28/32

Blow up the Southern cavern wall.

(Tal Tal Mountain Range)

Collected? ☐

Go back into the main part of the cave and head left, down the steps. Pull yourself across and then exit the cave.

Dash left, climb up, dodge the falling boulders, climb up, pick up the rocks, and under the top-right rock you'll find a **Secret Seashell**.

Secret Seashell 48/50

Under a rock, just past the falling boulders.

(Tal Tal Mountain Range)

Collected? ☐

Head left, open the chest for a **Purple Rupee**, then pick up the rock that's opposite the chest to reveal a set of steps going down. Use your magic powder on the lantern to **double your arrow carrying capacity**. Awesome!

Exit the cave, continue going left, drop down, go to the far left and pick up the **Heart Piece** here.

Heart Piece 29/32

Found to the left of the open gray rock area.

(Tal Tal Mountain Range)

Collected?

Now equip your bombs, go right, look up, and blow a hole in the Northern wall face. Head inside, hold up your Mirror Shield and walk up through the flames. Head up the steps, lift the rock by the exit to reveal a **Warp Point**, and continue left.

Equip your Shovel and look for four sets of stones with a clear patch of dirt in the middle. Dig this clear patch up to reveal a **Secret Seashell**.

Secret Seashell 49/50

Dig in middle of the four sets of stones.

(Tal Tal Mountain Range)

Collected?

Keep going left until you see the giant turtle rock. Equip your Ocarina and play the **Frog's song**. You'll trigger off an unexpected mini-boss battle of sorts.

The rock head will come to life and tries to attack you. The trick here is to stay close to the bottom wall and move out of the way as it tries to ram you. If its head hits the wall, it'll stun itself for a few seconds. Now's the time to drop a bomb by its head.

After three bombs breaks its rock cover off, the turtle head will rise up and attempt to ram you. You *do* need to be quicker on dodging it here as it's substantially faster at attacking you.

However, it's now vulnerable to your sword, so make sure to hit it as often as you can. Once it's defeated, head inside to begin the eighth – and final – major dungeon in the game...

101

Eighth Dungeon: Turtle Rock

Upon entering the dungeon, equip your boomerang and then head up. You'll come across a large, new enemy bat known as a **Vire**. Stun it with your boomerang and then attack it to split it into two smaller bats. Attack these bats and once they're gone, proceed through the left-hand door.

Watch out for the laser-shooting rotating eye as you attack the three snakes that are slithering around the room. Now quickly swap your boomerang for your bow and arrows, then head up to move into the next room.

Mini-Boss: Hinox

Fire off three arrows into this mini-boss to end the fight before it even really gets a chance to begin! Just be sure to keep some distance, otherwise Link takes heavy damage too.

In the next room you'll find a device that you can control the direction of with your joystick. The goal here is to push it left, then guide it up at the lit torch, then left at the top, and then immediately down to fill up the gap. Open the chest that appears for a **Red Rupee**.

Go down, jump across to the chest, and open it for a **Purple Rupee**. Now go left for the next mini-boss fight.

Mini-Boss: Spike Roller

You can use your boomerang here to cause multiple hits on each throw. If you throw it while close to the mini-boss, the boomerang passes through it (damaging it), then it passes back through on the way back. Combine that with a few sword swipes and this boss will be a goner in no time.

Go up, clear this room of enemies, pick up the **Small Key**, then go down two rooms and you now need to time your dashes very carefully as you have to get close to the Vacuum Mouth to dash towards the chest in the middle of the room. Inside you'll find the dungeon's **Compass**. Now walk into the Vacuum Mouth to be teleported back to the start of the dungeon (for a cheeky shortcut).

Go up, jump across the lava in front of you, and go up again. Go right, then guide the device to go up two squares and then left two squares. Run across the floor, equip your bombs, blow a hole in the wall, then push the top and bottom wooden blocks left one, then the middle block up one to reach the chest. Open the chest for this dungeon's **Map**. Now go up into the blown-up wall.

Go left, head down the steps, watch the timings of the lava and jump carefully across the platforms. Time your movement across the ladders as well, then climb up.

Get rid of every snake here to open the door. But be sure to open the chest in here for the **Stone Beak**.

Mini-Boss: Rover

Like before, lure it into throwing the ball at you. Now, very quickly, pick the ball up before the mini-boss does and throw it at the boss. Be sure to quickly pick the ball back up again (before the mini-boss does). Four hits with its own ball and it'll be a goner. Now go left.

The pattern for completing this floor with the device is:

Left, Up, Left, Up, Left three, Down, Right, Down, Right, Down, Right, Down, Right, Up, Right, Down, Right.

Pick up the **Small Key** that drops and plant a bomb in the middle of the Northern wall (where it's cracked).

In the next room, plant a bomb in the middle of the Western wall, walk left, then go up the steps that are beside the floating heart. Go down and then drop down into the room with the chest. Open the chest (ignoring the enemy inside), then proceed left.

Walk around the clay pots to the left-hand door and proceed through it. Jump up and across the lava pit to the exit at the top of the room.

Go right, and send the device up two, then right two, then up one (so it ends right in-between the two wooden blocks). Push the right-hand wooden block into the lava, then go up.

103

Open the metal block, go right, open up the door on the right, and then in the next room, jump over the Blade Traps and walk into the Link-shaped doorway at the top of the room.

Clear the next room of every enemy to open the locked door and head on through it. You need to be very quick and careful in this room as it's full of crumbling tiles. You need to keep moving from tile to tile as you attack the **Gibdos**. Once they're both gone, pick up the **Small Key** that drops by the entrance.

Dash left, ignore the two **Dodongo Snakes** here and keep going left. Jump across the lava, head up the steps, use the hookshot to pull yourself over to the chest and open it for some **Secret Medicine**.

Drop down, collect the floating items, go up the steps, go right, and at the top of the ladder, pull yourself across the lava gap to the tall ladder.

You'll reappear in the room filled with the Blade Traps. Go up once more, then plant a bomb in the middle of the left-hand wall. Walk through, use your magic powder on the unlit torch, jump across the gap, light the next torch, open up the metal block, then go left.

In the next room, get rid of the snake to open up the door. Light the torch in here, then plant a bomb in the middle of the left-hand wall.

Jump across the lava in the next room, equip your bow and arrows, then walk up onto the elevated platform at the bottom-middle of the room. Fire an arrow into the eye of the statue in front of you to cause a **Small Key** to drop down. Collect it, then go through the left-hand exit.

In this room, walk around to the block beside the chest, push it down, then walk back around to the chest again and push the block in front of the chest to the left. Open the chest for a **Small Key**. Head back through the right-hand exit.

Go up, then head up the steps at the top of this room to find yourself back outside. Head up the steps and pick up the **Heart Piece** from the grass.

Heart Piece 30/32

Outside, via the top of the N/W steps.

(Turtle Rock Dungeon)

Collected?

104

Continue right, activate the warp tile, then go back inside the dungeon once more.

Mini-Boss: Dodongo Snakes

Equip your bombs and throw them over the ledge and down to the ground so they land in front of one of the snakes. It'll take the snakes swallowing three bombs each before they're gone. Collect the **Small Key** from the chest that now appears. Now pull out your **Ocarina** and use the **Fish's song** to warp back to the dungeon's entrance.

Go back up, then jump North across the lava, and keep going North. Go right, then push the device up one, then right all the way across. Now dash right across the steps and all the way into the door on the far right.

Hit the crystal (turning it orange), then go left, up the steps at the bottom of the screen, go down, drop down to the open chest, continue left through the next room, go North, then right, send the device up three squares, then right, two, then up one so it ends in between the two wooden blocks once again.

Push the right-hand wooden block into the lava, go up, then right, and into the far right-hand door. Jump over the enemies, head up through the revolving door, now go through the blown-up wall on the left, jump across the gap, go left again, left once more, then go up the steps and unlock the metal block.

Use your hookshot to pull yourself across the gap to the wooden blocks beside the metal block, open the block, then head down the steps. This is a fairly simply 2D platforming section, so just take your time going right, and then climb up the tall ladder. When you reappear, drop down to begin a fight against a brand new mini-boss.

Mini-Boss: Blaino

The trick to defeating this tricky enemy is to charge your sword up and then jump up just as it starts its charged punching attack. If you time your jump correctly, you'll land just behind the mini-boss, allowing you to release your attack before it spins back around again. Don't worry if you don't make every hit count, this enemy is pretty fast. Just keep your cool, jump over it, and release your spin attack just as you land to maximize your odds of hitting it.

Once the battle's over, go up, open the chest, and grab a brand-new item! **The Magic Rod**!

105

The Magic Rod

The Magic Rod allows Link to fire off an infinite amount of fireballs that deals a similar level of damage to - most - enemies as the Koholint Sword. It can also be used to melt blocks of ice and light unlit torches!

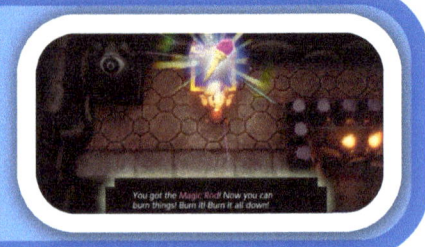

Now drop down, head down the steps, and go back the way you came.

After the 2D section, drop down from the ledge, go left, then continue left (through the blown-up wall), now head down through the South-Western exit in the room with the statue that you shot in the eye earlier.

Grab the hovering items, then push the third from the bottom wooden block into the lava. Jump across, dash right, then head down when you reach the middle.

Push the wooden block down into the lava, jump across the gap to your right, push the wooden block below you into the lava, go right, head up the steps, drop down off the ledge, go up the opposite set of steps, go down, drop off the ledge, go left, left again, now up, head right, and send the device up one square then all the way to the right.

Climb up the steps, then up the next set of steps beside it. Equip your magic rod and use it to get rid of the ice blocks in your way. However, when you see the ice blocks in front of the ledge and ladder, only destroy the upper row of ice blocks. Leave the bottom row alone so they act as a step up to the ladder.

Go down the two flights of steps and open up the locked door down here with your small key. Time for *another* mini-boss fight! (Well, it is the final dungeon in the game, what did you expect?)

Mini-Boss: Hydrosoar

You can keep this fight really simple by standing by the door you just came through. Let the mini-boss come to you, jump over it, quickly hit it from behind, and then immediately move up to the corner above you.

Hydrosoar will chase you up here, allowing you to, once again, jump over it and attack it from behind. Immediately head to the corner you just came from and repeat this pattern until the battle's over (which won't be long with your upgraded sword). Head up and get ready for another device moving puzzle.

If you make a mistake, just leave the room and re-enter it to reset the puzzle back to the start again.

Here's the directions in which you need to move the device:

Up 3, right 3, down 3, left 1, down 3, right, up, right, down, right, up 3, left 2, up 3, right 3, down 5, and right.

Open the chest that appears for the **Nightmare Key**. Leave, head right, then up the steps, go right, drop down, then up the steps, continue right, hookshot across to chest, and open it for a **Purple Rupee**.

Drop down, leave via the South-Western exit, dash down to the hovering items, push the third from bottom wooden block into the lava, jump across, dash right (to the middle), head down, push thew wooden block into the lava, jump right, push that wooden block down into the lava also, head up the steps, drop down the ledge, and then head up the steps in the top right-hand corner of the room.

Equip your magic rod and after using it to clear the ice here, jump across from the top central ledge to the gap on the left. Now drop down the ladder, shoot the bottom row of ice blocks away, move across to the ice block that's the second from the left and shoot upwards to clear the ice, creating a set of ice steps to the ladder.

Climb down the ladder, open the door to the boss room, and get ready to fight the boss and earn the eighth – and final – instrument needed.

Nightmare Boss Fight

As long as you dodge the fire and the boss as it bounces around the room, this is a very easy fight. Use your magic rod to fire shots into the middle of the room so the boss moves into the shots as it passes from side-to-side.

Once you hit it, keep the magic rod attacks up to get rid of the outer shell. It'll soon reveal its real face, and this is when you just keep attacking it with your magic rod as it bounces around the room and the battle will be over in a minute or two.

Collect the **Heart Container**, head up, and pick up the **Thunder Drum**. The final instrument you need to wake the Wind Fish!

108

Chapter 12

Before beating the final boss...

If want to finish the game with every Chamber Stone, Empty Bottle, Heart Piece, and Secret Seashell in the game, then it's time to tackle Dampé's Chamber Dungeons. You need to collect the remainder of the Chamber Stones first (this is because the remaining bottle, Heart Pieces and Secret Seashell require you to complete the dungeons first - which can only be unlocked with the appropriate Chamber Stone).

There's a total of **14** Chamber Stones that you can acquire as you travel around Koholint Island on your adventure.

If you're not bothered about collecting everything, then feel free to skip ahead to Chapter 13. Alright, still here? Great! Let's get to it then.

Chamber Stones 1 and 2

- Appears in the Trendy Game after completing the Catfish's Maw dungeon (fifth dungeon).

- Appears in the Trendy Game after completing the Item Trading Sub-Quest (end-game task).

Chamber Stones 3 - 9

Can be bought for a whopping **1,280 Rupees each** from the **Town Tool Shop**. That means you need to spend a total of **8,960 Rupees** to purchase all seven stones. You'll need each of these stones to unlock enough dungeon tiles to complete all of Dampé's dungeon challenges.

That's a wallet bursting amount of Rupees. So, here's our tips for farming as many Rupees as quickly (and hopefully as enjoyably) as possible. Pick the one that works the quickest for you (and, ideally, that you also find the most fun).

109

River Rapids

If you've reached this far and have become accurate and quick with the hookshot, then it's definitely possible to make a **200 Rupee profit** playing this game over and over. With a small amount of practice, you can beat this course in under 30-seconds (conveniently netting you a **Chamber Stone** for your efforts).

Make a Custom Dungeon

Visit Dampé's hut and use your tiles to create a custom dungeon that's been deliberately designed to contain almost nothing but treasure chests! Have fun optimizing the room placements and challenge yourself to building the most profitable custom dungeon around!

Trendy Game Pro

There's always a **Purple Rupee** worth **50 Rupees** waiting to be picked up. With each turn costing 10 Rupees, that leaves you with a *40 Rupee profit per play*. Simply leave the hut and re-enter to make it reappear. The added bonus with this method, is that it's very close to the Tool Town Shop, making the trip backwards and forwards relatively painless! Sweet!

Chamber Stones 10 and 11

- A reward for capturing an Ol' Baron.

- A reward for capturing an Ol' Baron that weighs more than 60 units.

Chamber Stones 12 and 13

- After collecting **30** Secret Seashells, step on the switch in the Secret Seashell Mansion for your reward.

- After collecting all **50** Secret Seashells, step on the switch in the Secret Seashell Mansion for your reward (as well as loads of Rupees!).

Chamber Stone 14

Your reward for beating the Rapids Race in *under 30 seconds*. If you can pull yourself around the course in this time, then use that skill to re-run the course and optimize your route for Rupee Farming. You can thank us later.

Chapter 13

The Final Challenge

You're almost there...

Once you exit the dungeon, take out your Ocarina and play **Mambo's Mambo**. Warp to **Dampé's Shack**, head down, and speak to Dampé who's standing by the wooden sign. Now go right and walk into his shack.

He'll take your Chamber Stones and create new chamber challenges with them. Select the "Arrange" option when prompted and you'll begin the first challenge. Complete each of the chambers to earn the reward noted.

You'll unlock more dungeon pieces to work with as you beat more regular dungeons (which is why we left this until after you beat the last regular dungeon).

Some dungeons will be partially started for you (such as the early ones) and others you are required to build from scratch (and could be multiple floors in size).

Each challenge dungeon introduces a new element that must be used for the challenge to be completed successfully. We'll take you through every challenge and show you how to build and finish them with ease.

Here's a few tips and tricks that will help you before you begin building:

- Chests will first contain Small Keys and won't change to Rupees until you've collected every Small Key required to beat that dungeon.

- Dampé replenishes your bombs and arrows before you start a dungeon.

Secret Seashell 50/50

Complete first four Chamber Challenges.

(Dampe's Shack)

Collected?

Heart Piece 31/32

Complete the "Fill up your heart" challenge.

(Dampe's Shack)

Collected?

Heart Piece 32/32

Complete "Passageway Central" challenge.

(Dampe's Shack)

Collected?

- If the game won't let you place a piece down, press Y to see what the error is.

- You need an equal number of doors (including the door that requires a Nightmare Key) to be able to finish building your dungeon.

Complete the "**Heart Shortage**" chamber to earn a new **Chamber Stone** and the final **Fairy Bottle**!

Complete the "**Ticking Clock**" chamber to earn a new **Chamber Stone**, the final **Heart Container**, and a **+Wallmasters Effect**! Sweet!

Once you've earned the rewards above, you can keep going, or you can leave. Your choice. Once you're ready to leave, head back outside, (and as long as you have found all 50 Secret Seashells), warp to Seashell Mansion and stand on the switch. You'll be rewarded with a bunch of Rupees and a **Chamber Stone**.

Step outside and warp to **Ukuku Prairie**. Now go to Madame CiaoCiao's house and place the CiaoCiao figure on the wooden plaque on the table.

Side Mission: Trendy Figures

It's now time to finish off this side-mission. The goal is to pick up a toy figure from the Trendy Game shop in Mabe Village and place it on a plaque in a specific location (which are all found in Mabe Village).

So, we'll list the figures in the order you can grab them and where they need to go. Simply return back to the Trendy Game for ever new figure until you reach the end.

- **Goomba**: Top table in Marin's home.

- **Spiny**: On the right-hand table in the green home.

- **Boo**: On the central round table in the green home.

- **Cheep Cheep**: By the door in the purple roofed house (directly west of the Trendy Game).

- **Blooper**: On the top table in the purple roofed house (directly west of the Trendy Game).

- **Shy Guy**: On the floor by the right entrance in the green home.

- **Piranha Plant**: At the bottom of the beds in Marin's home.

- **Pokey**: On the floor in the top-left corner of the green home.

En-route to the Egg

Head to the library in Mabe Village and read the book in the bottom right-hand corner. As you have the magnifying lens, you **MUST** read this book to get the route you must take to make it through the egg and to the game's final boss.

Note

The route in the book is different for *every* playthrough. Therefore, we strongly recommend that you make a note of the path somewhere - you'll need it again soon!

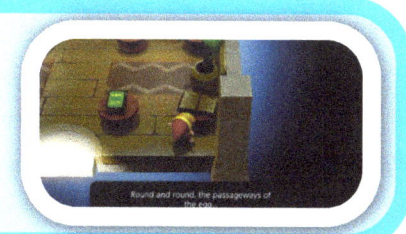

Step outside the library and warp to **Dampé's Shack**. When you arrive, immediately go left, lift up the rocks by the wooden sign, go right, climb the ladder up to **Mt. Tamaranch**. Equip your **Ocarina** and select Marin's **Ballad of the Windfish** song. Dash up to the egg at the top and play Marin's song to open up the entrance to the egg.

Final Dungeon: The Wind Fish's Egg

Dash forwards and then fall down into the gaping chasm below. Head up and you'll enter the maze-like belly of the egg.

Equip your feather and your magic powder and follow the route that you found at the library earlier (and that you, hopefully, wrote down like we recommended you should earlier!).

Note: If you make a mistake, you need to restart the path from the beginning.

Final Boss: Shadow Nightmare

This is it, the final battle. The final boss takes on five different forms. Thankfully, we've helped guide you this far, so we can definitely help you get to the end and earn that coveted no-death ending. Are you ready?

Shadow Nightmare: Form 1

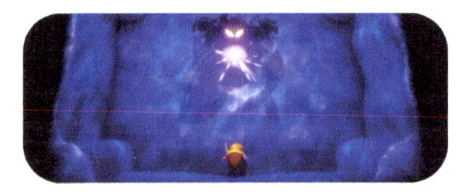

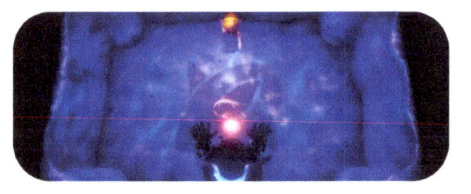

Wait for the blob-like form to jump and land near you. Immediately throw some magic powder on it to damage the boss. Three hits of your magic powder will start phase two of this battle.

Shadow Nightmare: Form 2

If you've ever played against Ganon in another Zelda game, then this classic take on ping pong will be second nature to you. Stand at the opposite end of the room to the boss and swing your sword at the ball of energy it fires at you.

114

If you time your swipe right, the sword will deflect the ball of energy back towards the boss. Repeat this for a total of four times.

However, if you see the boss fire a series of small blue balls at you, dodge these as you can't hit them back!

Shadow Nightmare: Form 3

For this phase, charge up your sword and your goal is to attack the yellow eyes on the tail of the boss as it moves around the room (it's basically a repeat of the Moldorm boss fight from the first dungeon).

Be careful though, as the boss speeds up significantly each time you hit it. It requires three strikes on the tail to send it to the next form.

Shadow Nightmare: Form 4

You can get a head start on this fight by performing a spinning attack on the boss, just as it changes form, after it moves to the middle of the room. This will get an easy hit in for you. You really want to hit the boss with spinning attacks too.

However, when you see it spinning its pole around, run down to one of the bottom corners and run from left to right when it fires the fire-bats at you.

This form requires three solid strikes to send it to its next form.

Shadow Nightmare: Form 5

Equip your **Magic Rod**, head to the bottom-left corner of the room and use the magic rod to strike the boss. If you stand in this location, the boss will keep attacking you from the same angle, making this phase much easier. You need to hit the boss in this form a total of eight times.

Shadow Nightmare: Final Form (Dethl)

Alright, it's time for the boss' final form. Quickly equip your bow and arrows and get ready to perform multiple jumps over its spinning arms as the cross your path. The goal here is to watch for the eye opening in the middle and fire off as many arrows into its eyes as you can before it closes again.

You need to land a solid six arrows in its eyes to beat the boss. Simply walk up the steps that appear to finish the game and begin the well-earned, and emotionally charged, ending.

Hopefully, you haven't got a death registered on your save file, so you can watch the special ending scene.

CONGRATULATIONS! You've completed the game!

But, have you managed to finish the game without dying to unlock that secret ending?...

Chapter 14

Secrets and Easter Eggs

Link's Awakening was home to a lot of cool secrets and Easter eggs when it originally released on the Gameboy in 1993. The Switch remake carries most of these across, while also adding in a few more that are unique to this version...

Hidden Music

Changing your character's name on the save file screen will unlock some hidden musical melodies for you to listen to. Try out each of these names for yourself:

- Zelda
- Marin
- Totakeke
- Moyse

Bomb Arrows

Another trick that's been carried over since the original 1993 (and DX) releases, if you equip your bow and arrows and your bombs and then press both action buttons at the same time, you'll fire off an arrow with a bomb attached to it!

Once the arrow hits a wall, the bomb will explode. This is actually very handy for getting rid of enemies that are far away, or even for hitting colored switches earlier than you're supposed to in dungeons! Definitely worth trying. It's a lot of fun!

Death by a Thousand Pecks

In Mabe Village, you'll see a number of Cuccos flapping around. If you hit one around 35 times, it'll call out to its Cucco friends who'll now dash in and will keep pecking you until you run out of health! You can reset this onslaught by entering a building.

THIEF!

Probably one of the coolest Easter eggs in Link's Awakening is the ability to steal an item from inside the Town Tool Shop in Mabe Village (and was also in the original Gameboy version).

If you pick up an item (preferably a high-priced item), run around the shop keeper, and if you're quick enough to go through the exit before he turns back around to face you (an is is harder to do in the remake), then the game will let you know that you got it for free.

However, because choices have consequences, every character in the game will refer to you as THIEF! From now on (on this save file). Also, if you decide to go back into the Town Tool Shop? Well... you're in for a shocking surprise (resulting in a death on your save file).

Therefore, it's recommended that you try this out for fun and then exit the game without saving!

Cameos

There's a load of characters in the game that have made an appearance in a Nintendo game in one form or another over the years. Let's take a look at them:

- **Tarin**: (aka: Mario).

- **Henhouse Keeper**: (aka: Luigi).

- **Mr. Write**: From Sim City on the SNES.

- **Princess Peach**: The photo that's in the letter that you give to Mr. Write.

- **Chain Chomp**: Mario games.

- **Sea Urchins**: (AKA: Gordos) Kirby games.

- **Kirby**: Found in Eagle Tower.

- **Yoshi**: Mario games.

- **Wart**: The Dream King in Super Mario Bros. 2 (USA and European versions).

- **Shy Guys**: Mario games.

- **Goombas**: Mario games.

- **Piranha Plants**: Mario games.

- **Boo**: Mario games.

- **Thwomps**: Mario games.

- **Cheep-Cheeps**: Mario games.

- **Bloopers**: Mario games.

- **Bob-ombs**: Mario games.

- **Pokeys**: Mario games,

- **Prince Richard**: Japanese Gameboy game "*Kaeru no Tame ni Kane wa Naru*" (which, when roughly translated, means "*For the Frog the Bells Toll*" (hence all the frogs in his house).

Hidden Marin Dialogue

During the part of the game where Marin is following behind you, there's a lot of hidden dialogue and secret cut-scenes that Marin will only reveal when you are in certain locations or do certain actions. These are:

- After Marin joins you, head to the far-left corner of the beach then head South to the bottom of the narrow walkway to trigger a hidden scene.

  - Watch how her empathy for the poor chicken changes after hitting a Cucco more than 20 times...

  - Fall into the well in Mabe Village and Marin lands on top of you.

  - Look inside the wooden drawers in Marin's house.

- Pick up, and then break, a jar in front of her.

- Equip your shovel and start digging while outside.

- Play the "Ballad of the Wind Fish" song that she taught you to get her feedback.

- Take her into the Trendy Game shop in Mabe Village for a very entertaining secret!

- Try and take Marin into a dungeon with you.

- She makes a comment if you come back from the dungeon with some lost health.

- However, if you come out of the dungeon with only half a heart left, she'll say something else instead.

- Take Marin to see the Chef Bear in Animal Village.

Fun with the Magic Powder

Throwing some magic powder onto certain enemies or characters will reveal some cool hidden responses. Try throwing some powder on:

- Buzz blobs.

- The skull sitting in an alcove in the South-Eastern side of the desert.

- The lonely grave that's surrounded by purple flowers (the ghost's grave).

- Gibdos.

- Sparks.

Relived Nightmares

When you reach the end of the game and fight off against the multiple different forms of the final boss, pay very close attention to the shape that the boss forms in each phase. They're based off of a different boss Link has fought in different Zelda games. How many can you figure out?

Say Cheese!

There was exclusive content released only on the Gameboy Color release of Link's Awakening DX. Where Dampé's hut stands in the Switch remake, there was a camera shop run by a mouse!

He asks you if you wish to have your photo taken. There's a total of **12** photos that you can trigger (some of which are time sensitive and can be easily missed), so let's take a look at each of them in turn, along with how to trigger each one.

What makes this extra special is that, if you attach a Gameboy Printer to your Gameboy Color, you could physically print out these photos directly from the printer!!! How awesome is that?!

"Here stands a brave man" or "Game Over!"

Requirements: Roc's Feather

Taken upon entering the Camera shop. The first photo is taken if you answer "Yes", the second if you keep answering "No."

"Ocean View"

Requirements: First photo and be with Marin

Once you've spoken with Marin by the water's edge (but before you head to Yarna Desert), take Marin to the South-Western corner of the beach and walk down to the very bottom.

"Heads Up!"

Requirements: (Time Sensitive) First photo and be with Marin

After taking Marin to the beach spot above, take her to the spot in **Mabe Village** where you had to drop down into the hole to collect the Heart Piece to trigger this photo opportunity (how did the mouse even get in there in the first place!?).

"Camera Hog"

Requirements: (Time Sensitive) First photo and be with Marin

After taking Marin to the cave (and dusting yourself off), take her to the weather vane in the village. The mouse will offer to take a photo of both of you. At least, that was the plan until a certain someone decides to photobomb the picture!

Take a look at Link and Marin's faces in the photo!!!

"Link discovers Ulrira's Secret"

Requirements: First photo

Visit Ulrira's house in Mabe Village and walk up to the window by the door. The mouse will then take a cool photo of Ulrira chatting away!

"Link plays with BowWow"

Requirements: First photo and BowWow is back home

After getting BowWow back home, approach the wooden stake to trigger the photographer. He'll egg you on to get closer and closer, until BowWow starts chasing after Link when he gets too close! So much for saving him from the Moblins!

"THIEF!"

Requirements: First photo

The THIEF! Easter Egg goes one step further in the DX version. The mouse will let you run away with your ill-gotten gains, while taking a perfectly framed shot of your illegal activities. Busted!

"Can't Swim?"

Requirements: First photo and the Hookshot

Once you've acquired the Hookshot, head to where the fisherman under the bridge is sitting. Jump onto his boat and chat to him. This triggers off a funny scene where the fisherman pulls up the mouse from the water!

"I found Zora"

Requirements: First photo and Magnifying Lens

Once you've finished the item trade side-quest and acquired the Magnifying Lens, go to Animal Village and go into the top right-hand house and speak with the Zora there for a photo.

"A regal home"

Requirements: (**Very** Time Sensitive) First photo, Power Bracelet, and closed castle gates

Your only chance to get this photo is before the gates to Kanalet Castle are opened. Visit the front of the castle before you begin the quest for the Golden Leaves for the photo.

"I was very afraid"

Requirements: First photo and ghost returned to their grave

Take the ghost back to their grave and then re-approach the gravestone once more to trigger the photo, this time with a much happier ghost.

"Close call (Almost too close)"

Requirements: First photo, Feather, Bracelet, and Flippers (but **without** the flying rooster)

Go four screens to the right from the green hut. Clear the bridge on the far right to trigger the final photo opportunity...

Chapter 15

Hearts and Seashell locations

All 32 Heart Piece Locations

30/32 Page 104
28/32 Page 100
12/32 Page 55
29/32 Page 101
31+32 Page 112
09/32 Page 50
03/32 Page 30
27/32 Page 93
02/32 Page 22
06/32 Page 35
24/32 Page 89
25/32 Page 90
05/32 Page 34
08/32 Page 43
26/32 Page 91
01/32 Page 15
04/32 Page 32
23/32 Page 88
07/32 Page 38

124

13/32
Page 60

22/32
Page 84

21/32
Page 83

14/32
Page 51

15/32
Page 61

20/32
Page 82

17/32
Page 65

11/32
Page 54

19/32
Page 73

10/32
Page 53

18/32
Page 67

16/32
Page 63

125

All 50 Secret Seashell Locations

- 47/50 Page 99
- 46/50 Page 99
- 45/50 Page 97
- 43/50 Page 93
- 44/50 Page 94
- 17/50 Page 55
- 18/50 Page 60
- 33/50 Page 83
- 32/50 Page 78
- 37/50 Page 86
- 34/50 Page 84
- 04/50 Page 35
- 31/50 Page 76
- 30/50 Page 75
- 19/50 Page 62
- 09/50 Page 50
- 38/50 Page 87
- 27/50 Page 67
- 29/50 Page 73
- 28/50 Page 72
- 21/50 Page 62
- 20/50 Page 62
- 15/50 Page 54
- 14/50 Page 53

127

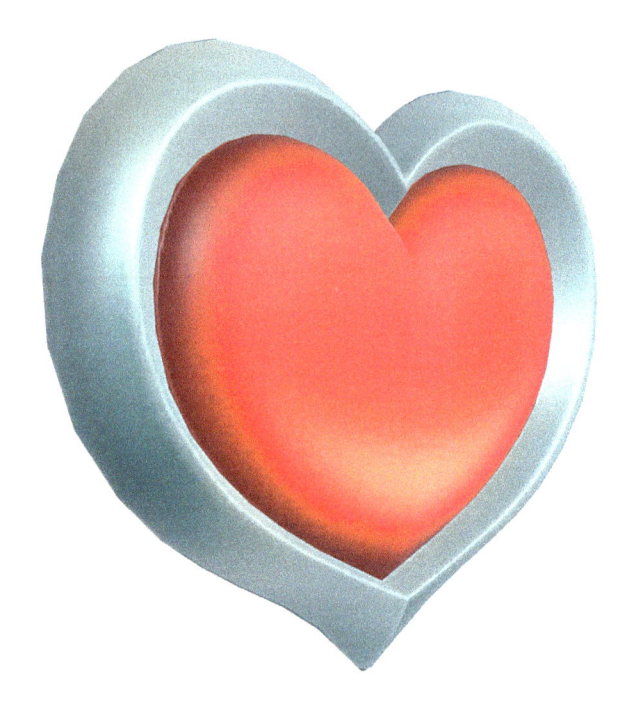

*We truly hope our guide has helped you
and that you have enjoyed using it.*

If possible, please remember to leave a review.

Best wishes, Alpha Strategy Guides